GIRL WITH
A SNIPER
RIFLE

Lady Death
The Memoirs of Stalin's Sniper
Lyudmila Pavlichenko
ISBN: 978–1–78438–270–4

Red Army Sniper
A Memoir of the Eastern Front in World War II
Yevgeni Nikolaev
ISBN: 978–1–78438–236–0

Eastern Front Sniper
The Life of Matthäus Hetzenauer
Roland Kaltenegger
ISBN: 978–1–78438–216–2

Snipers at War
An Equipment and Operations History
John Walter
ISBN: 978–1–78438–184–4

The Sniper Encyclopaedia
An A–Z Guide to World Sniping
John Walter
ISBN: 978–1–78438–240–7

GIRL WITH A SNIPER RIFLE

An Eastern Front Memoir

Yulia Zhukova

Foreword by
Martin Pegler

Translated by
David Foreman

GREENHILL BOOKS

Girl with a Sniper Rifle
This English-language edition
first published in 2019 by
Greenhill Books,
c/o Pen & Sword Books Ltd,
47 Church Street, Barnsley,
S. Yorkshire, S70 2AS

www.greenhillbooks.com
contact@greenhillbooks.com

ISBN: 978–1–78438–398–5

First published in Russia in 2006 by
Tsentrpoligraf, Moscow

CIP data records for this title are available from the British Library

Printed and bound in the UK by TJ International, Padstow
Designed and typeset by Donald Sommerville

Typeset in 12/16 pt Minion Pro

Contents

Plates

Myself aged sixteen.

My parents, Alexandra Ivanovna and Konstantin Sergeyevich Zhukov, in the 1930s.

My friend, Meritorious Artist of the Karelian–Finnish Autonomous Republic the talented singer Taisia Kulchitskaya.

The way we looked on arrival at Sniper School: myself, Roza Vozina, Anna Astrova and Valentina Shipova, 10 April 1944.

Our platoon, with Platoon Commander Second Lieutenant Mazhnov, May 1944.

Our squad, with Sergeant Masha Duvanova, August 1944.

With my new sniper's rifle and my friend Lyuba Ruzhitskaya, June 1944.

With Platoon Commander Irina Papikhina and Squad Commander Masha Duvanova prior to departure for the front, November 1944.

A farewell photo with Company Sergeant-Major Masha Logunova.

A studio portrait with my mother, November 1944.

The building near Silikatnaya station in which the Sniper School was located.

Map of the 88th Rifle Division's progress westward.

With Vasily Stolbov, Pyotr Chirkov and Alexei Popov. Geidau, East Prussia, 20 June 1945.

After I was presented with my medal 'For Bravery'.

With Masha Duvanova in 1975.

Sniper School graduates in Red Square during our 1975 reunion.

My old squad, seen at our first reunion in 1975.

My Red Army booklet.

My Sniper School graduation certificate.

My Army cap and epaulettes.

My awards of the war and post-war periods.

Enjoying the company of my family: with my great-granddaughter Margarita, granddaughter Varvara and daughter Olga, Victory Day 2018.

Foreword

I doubt that anyone who reads this book by Yulia Konstantinovna Zhukova will have heard of her. She was not a high-scoring sniper like Ludmila Pavlichenko, or a poster-girl like Rosa Shanina, but one of the hundreds of anonymous women snipers whose stories did not make newspaper headlines but who contributed materially to the defeat of the invading German armies.

Zhukova came from a staunchly patriotic Soviet family and she volunteered to work in an engineering factory as soon as she left school. In late 1944 she went to the Central Women's Sniper School in Moscow, from which she graduated and was promptly sent to the East Prussian front. There, her official tally as a sniper for the war was eight, although as she correctly points out, reality and official figures often varied widely. This could make the reader ask how her experiences were worthy of an entire book. But that would be to miss the essence of what is a truly fascinating account of the experiences of a very young girl caught up in what was arguably the was most savage and bestial fighting on any front since the middle ages. Despite her extensive sniper training, she was later transferred to a howitzer regiment in an infantry role, where she was the only woman. She had no privacy and was constantly molested, not by her own comrades who were fiercely protective of her, but by senior officers, who regarded the availability of women soldiers almost as a perk of rank.

Of equal interest is the continuation of her story in the hard post-war years, when she suffered from post-traumatic stress for 30 years in the form of terrible nightmares, and a total mental block about her past. Her first regimental reunion in 1975 was not only to open the floodgates of repressed memory but also effect a form of therapy, and she was finally able to acknowledge with pride the part she played in the defence of her homeland. Bearing in mind the extraordinary age at which she began writing her memoir, it is fascinating not only for the detail in which she covers her training and combat experience, but how she coped with being a woman in an almost exclusively male environment. It is a quite remarkably open and honest account of war as seen from the viewpoint of a naive girl of eighteen, but with the hindsight of a mature woman who despite everything, went on to become a successful head teacher, a wife and mother. Most impressively, Zhukova writes without blame or rancour, and is even happy to correct her story when evidence in the form of long-forgotten letters she wrote were produced that contradicted her memory.

This is one of the very best memoirs of the Great Patriotic War that I have read, and I congratulate Yulia Zhukova and the publishers on producing a quite outstanding work.

Martin Pegler

Preface to the English Edition

Today I turned ninety-two years of age. I am sitting in my study in front of a computer and recalling how much time I spent here when I was working on my reminiscences of the war and how hard that book was for me to write.

It is now over seventy years since the war ended, but it is still alive within me, a disturbing and exciting presence. I would very much like to forget it, to banish from my memory the horrors I experienced as an eighteen-year-old girl.

I remember that, when I returned home from the front in August 1945, the first thing I did was to destroy almost everything that could remind me about it, even the letters I had written to my parents from the front and those which front-line friends had sent to me. All that remained were a forage cap, some epaulettes and a few photographs; I could not bring myself to dispose of them. I never gave talks about my reminiscences, never took part in military sports, and I only put on my military decorations for the first time thirty years after the war was over.

Relatives and friends repeatedly asked me to write just a little about what had happened to me, even just for those who were close to me, but I refused, because I did not want to recall all that, to find myself once again plunged into war. It all turned out to be in vain; the war remained alive within me. I was tormented by nightmares, which were repeated over many years: retreat, encirclement, capture. I did not know how to get rid of them.

But in 1975, on the thirtieth anniversary of victory, there was a reunion in Moscow for graduates of all four courses run at the Central Women's Sniping School, and this was followed by a reunion for veterans of the 31st Army, in which I had served. Listening to addresses by my friends from the front line, I thought for the first time: why should I not write my memoirs? But I realised how difficult it would be to do this, because I had forgotten a lot and had no experience as a writer, and I abandoned the idea as unrealistic.

Then these reunions became regular events and every one of them was like a celebration. It sounds strange to say it, but perhaps these reunions with front-line friends slightly blunted the sharp edge of my memories about the war, and I began to accept them more calmly.

But then a catastrophe occurred: the country which we loved and had defended ceased to exist; it split into fifteen independent states corresponding to the union republics of the USSR. And those of us who had yesterday stood shoulder to shoulder in the trenches as regimental mates, defending a common homeland, became citizens of different countries that were not always friendly to one another. This was very difficult to get over.

But in October 1998, in yet another anti-Soviet broadcast, a well-known Russian television host rudely insulted the entire older generation. A wave of indignation swept through society; there was a flood of lawsuits. But neither the authorities nor the courts reacted to this outburst. War veterans in general were having a very difficult time altogether, both materially and in terms of morale. And I realised that now I was simply obliged to write about our generation and the harsh times in which we lived. It didn't matter how it turned out, it seemed to me; the main thing was to tell the truth. The writing proved very difficult. Many events and facts were hard to bring to mind. At times the faces of my dead regimental comrades would appear before me and I really sensed the sounds, colours and smells of wartime. I became nervous and it appeared as if I was experiencing those events once again. Seeing the state I was in, relatives urged me to abandon the work, but I could no longer stop myself. I wanted to tell everything right to the end in memory of my front-line friends. The result was this book, to which I originally gave a different title – 'For the Sake of Remembrance'. Then, after consulting with my granddaughter Varvara, I gave it its present title – 'Girl with a Sniper Rifle'.

In recent times much has changed for the better in our country. Attitudes to war veterans have also changed and evaluations of the Soviet people's role in the defeat of German fascism have become more objective. Some old museums dealing with the war are being restored and new ones established, memoirs by war veterans are being published, and both feature and documentary films about the war are being released. Enthusiasm for military and patriotic ideals is on the rise and greater attention is devoted to educating young people in a spirit of patriotism (the cadet movement is being revived in schools and anniversaries of major World War II battles are observed). A few years ago, we saw the birth of the practice of celebrating Victory Day, 9 May, by holding triumphal marches around the main streets and squares of our towns and cities, bearing portraits of grandfathers, fathers and mothers who took part in the war. This movement was given the name 'The Immortal Regiment' and millions of people of all ages took part; whole families would go out onto the streets.

In recent years I find myself more and more frequently recalling the day when we learned that the war was over. How we celebrated! We were young and naïve and we firmly believed that this was the last war on earth, that people who had endured so much grief, lost friends, family, and children, would not want to repeat this horror and would always live in peace and harmony.

And we were proud of having contributed to the achievement of peace on earth.

We were mistaken. Peace did not descend on the earth following World War II. Now, when I learn that fascism is being revived in some countries and bloody conflicts are breaking out again in some places and people are dying, I remember the millions of people who perished in that war. What were those sacrifices made for? For me today my participation in that war is a source of both pain and pride; any lies told about the events of those years cause me anguish. And I always experience a feeling of shame for those politicians, scholars, and members of the media and the intelligentsia who deliberately distort the course and results of the Second World War, try to dethrone true heroes and impose on society new ones of sometimes dubious provenance, insulting the memory of those who perished and humiliating surviving veterans, of whom few remain. And it is offensive to see monuments to soldiers who crushed fascism being torn down.

With every passing year there are fewer and fewer of us left who took part in the Great War for the Fatherland. It is no bad thing that many have left behind recollections, documents and photographs recording those events.

I am glad that my book of memoirs is being published in Britain, which was our ally in those years in the fight against German fascism.

I would like to hope that, after reading this book, readers will learn something new about my country and its people, about the bloodiest war in human history, and perhaps simply look at some events in a different way.

Yulia Zhukova
26 February 2018

Dedicated to my beloved girls,
my daughter Olga
and granddaughter Varvara.

Introduction

I never thought of writing my memoirs, and always considered that it was just the prerogative of exceptional people who had achieved something significant, important. So, when it was suggested that I write about myself and my times, it struck me as an unnecessary undertaking. However, the idea gradually got the better of me. I began to believe that any person's life is of interest insofar as he or she is a reflection of his or her time – a witness, or even a participant, in significant historical events. That aside, it is very important, I think, that future generations should have a better knowledge of the way their forebears lived, what they occupied themselves with, what they thought about, and how they viewed the times they lived in.

I decided to start writing. Chronologically my life coincided with a very interesting period in the history of my country; I had witnessed and endured a great deal.

I became a participant in one of the most tragic but greatest events of the twentieth century – the Great War for the Fatherland. My work in the Young Communist League coincided with a period of many creative youth initiatives. And I devoted almost thirty-nine years to my beloved cause – education of the people.

I recall both the repressions of the 1930s and the wide-scale campaign of the 1950s to denounce Stalin's personality cult. I became a witness of the process whereby a great power – the

USSR – was left in ruins and turned into a country of semi-colonial status. My life is, as it were, divided into two epochs.

I always served my Soviet homeland and my people honourably. I never sought an easy path or personal advantage in life, and always strove to help people. My country's current tragedy is also my own personal tragedy, because I never divorced my own personal fate from that of my country.

I am not ashamed of my life. I can boldly look people in the eye.

If I were asked to formulate briefly what my life was like, I would put it like this: 'The history of my life is a tiny particle of the history of my generation.'

When I recall the most important, the main thing, in my life, then I think first and foremost of the war years. For me everything connected with the war is both very hard to face but also very sacred. My participation in the war is a source of both pain and pride to me. All through the subsequent years I strove to forget about the war, but my memory constantly took me back to those distant times.

Today a lot of truth and a lot of untruth is written about the war. I always felt insulted when some scholars, writers, journalists and film-makers, inspired by some malicious glee and passion (especially in the 1990s), falsified the history of the Great War for the Fatherland, belittled the role of the Soviet Union in the defeat of Nazi Germany, and humiliated and insulted those who achieved victory in the war years 1941–5. I once read a remark by the writer Konstantin Paustovsky: 'There is nothing more loathsome than a man's indifference to his own country, to its past, present and future, to its language, way of life . . . and people.'

It was my lot both to endure the difficulties of wartime in the rear and to taste the soldier's tribulations at the front. Today I feel obliged, inasmuch as I am able, to write honestly and frankly about that tragic but heroic time. I will simply write – without embellishment, and also without laying it on too thick – how I experienced those events, what I felt, and what my comrades, my kith and kin and I actually did.

I once read a letter in a newspaper from a rank and file soldier who had gone through the entire war without once being wounded. He wrote that he had not done anything heroic at the front, had not been decorated, but had simply carried out his soldier's duties in an honourable way. And he went on to stress that he was proud of his fate, of the fact that during his homeland's most arduous days he was in the trenches, on the front line.

I share the viewpoint of this unknown soldier and subscribe to his letter.

It is my wish that there should be more young people among my readers; in the hands of our youth lies the future of the country, for whose freedom and very existence many millions of Soviet people gave their lives.

CHAPTER 1

Beginnings

I shall never forget 22 June 1941.

On that day the leader of our Pioneer* squad, Yulia Kovalenko, was leaving to spend the school holidays with relatives in the Ukraine. She was in the ninth class, had spent two years in our squad and always given us a great deal of her attention, often dashing into our seventh-grade classroom, even during school breaks, while her friends were discussing their concerns and problems. Yulia was a very good-looking girl – tall, statuesque, with hair in a thick, brown braid, big grey-blue eyes and thick black eyebrows. We were all very fond of our squad leader and therefore decided we must go to the station to see her off and say goodbye till the start of the next school year. However, we kept our intentions secret; we wanted to surprise her.

At around 10 or 11 o'clock we gathered near the school. School No. 1, which we attended, provided education from the fifth to the tenth grade. It was situated on the main street of Uralsk [now also known as Oral, in Kazakhstan], Soviet Street, and comprised a two-storey brick building, housing just eight classrooms, four above and four below, as well as an assembly hall which doubled as a gym. It was an old school, dilapidated and poorly equipped.

---

* The Pioneers were a Communist Party youth organisation with some similarities to the Scouts.

On the other hand, the teaching contingent was outstanding. Every year the majority of our school-leavers gained entry into leading colleges in Moscow, Leningrad, Saratov and other major cities. There was no private coaching back then, so this success was due to our teachers. From what I heard from my Uncle Misha (Mikhail Ivanovich Sinodaltsev, my mother's brother), a wonderful maths teacher, I know that the examiners at higher institutes often asked our school-leavers where and at whose hands they had gained such brilliant knowledge. Besides, the atmosphere at our school was always very warm and stood out for its friendliness and respect for the pupils. We loved our school, spent a lot of our free time there and, if we were gathering to go somewhere together, we would invariably meet near the school.

Such was the case on that day; we had gathered at the usual place. It was a magnificent day – fine, warm, and unusually sunny. Everything was bright and cheerful. We had just completed seven years of schooling and ahead lay the long summer holidays. And as well as that we were imagining how glad and surprised our beloved squad leader would be when she saw her squad members at the station almost in full array. We were laughing and joking.

Then suddenly a woman came up to us with tears in her eyes: 'Children, where are you off to? The war's started!' Her words seemed to us to be so absurd that we did not even pay any attention to them; they somehow slipped past without affecting any of us. We laughed and joked about the strange weeping woman.

Uralsk was quite a small provincial city; you could easily cross it completely on foot. There was no local public transport at all as far as I remember. Our merry throng headed for the station. There we repeatedly heard the words: 'The war's started!' The platform was all a-bustle: people were crying or shouting something, and there was a feeling of general tension in the air. Now we believed it – misfortune really had come our way.

Our mood slumped and we all kind of drooped. Yulia did not go anywhere. We headed back to town with her and her family and went home.

Of course, back then we still did not fully understand the nature of the war that had descended on us, how serious it was, how long it would last, what a tragedy it would be for our country and how many lives it would cost. But I well remember that everyone I knew or socialised with was firmly confident that we were bound to be victorious.

At home it was all gloom and tears. I sat down at the table and with an ordinary black pencil drew a poster: Red Army soldiers with rifles, tanks behind them and aeroplanes above them. And an inscription: 'The Nazis will not get through!' I stuck it on the wall above the table with drawing pins. It was, no question, a crude poster, but for some reason nobody wanted to take it down, and it hung there for a long time. Maybe because the inscription voiced the general mood.

A new life began that was completely unlike my previous one. Somehow, imperceptibly, everything changed, and our whole lifestyle became different. But my deepest impression of those first few days is of huge crowds of people near the town enlistment office, the city's Party committee headquarters and the city centre of the Young Communist League committee. Everyone was bursting to get to the front. Both I and friends from my class looked enviously on those departing there, but realised that the army would not take us at the age of fifteen. Therefore, we would sometimes meet and think: what can we do, how can we help the country?

At the same time, first my father and then my mother also tried to get to the front. Dad was turned down because his right eye was missing; he had lost it while helping to crush the Menshevik revolt* in the Caucasus and he now wore a glass eye. Then he tried to join the partisans and even acquired a short overcoat of grey soldier's cloth. But once again he was barred for the same reason. My mother was rejected because I was still a minor and, at the beginning of the war, this was taken into consideration.

A huge number of military personnel arrived in our town; the summer military college was transferred here from Voroshilovgrad (now Lugansk, Ukraine). The cadets would march around in formation (so beautifully!), singing, and passers-by on the pavement would stop, wave, and call out to them, while women would wipe away their tears. Little boys would march in a gang behind them, envying them and their attractive uniforms, dreaming of being like them.

Then the No. 231 factory, which was named after Marshal Voroshilov and manufactured naval mines and torpedoes, was evacuated from Leningrad to Uralsk. It was re-sited in three areas: at Zaton (a river inlet 12 kilometres from the city), in the former city auto-repair workshops, and at the polytechnic college. We saw the huge, cumbersome equipment being transported to the factory. There were not enough trucks – they had also been mobilised for the front – so the carrying was done by horses and camels. At the site where the new factory was being set up there was constant rumbling, knocking and scraping night and day. And soon, within a month or a month and a half, columns of vehicles covered with tarpaulins and caravans of horses and camels were to be seen emerging from there – carrying the factory's production. The time spans within which the factory was in essence built anew and manufacturing commenced were simply fantastic. I realised this only later, when I began to work there and saw the scale of what had been achieved.

---

* The Mensheviks were a minority Socialist group, rivals of the Bolsheviks. The Mensheviks established a regime in Georgia but this was overthrown by the Bolsheviks in 1921.

Then another factory arrived. With each enterprise came specialists, other workers, and their families. They all needed somewhere to live. A so-called process of 'concentration' began – the new arrivals were accommodated in the apartments and private houses of the Uralsk locals. What staggers me most of all today is that people did not only not object or show indignation at this, but actually offered to take evacuees; sometimes they even went to the station and brought back families to their own homes. Today this is difficult to imagine, but back then it seemed natural.

We had nobody billeted with us. We lived at that time with my mother's other brother, Uncle Sasha (Alexander Ivanovich Sinodaltsev). Uncle Sasha was a very gentle and good-natured man. At the same time, I remember him as a convinced Communist and patriot. He worked for the police and had a two-room apartment, which was a rarity back then. The three of us were huddled in a small room 3 metres by 3.8, while Uncle Sasha, his wife and son lived in the other one, which was a bit more spacious. There was nowhere to accommodate anyone else but I recall feeling sorry that our family could not take anybody.

We soon caught a glimpse of the first refugees – skinny, grimy, no light in their eyes. It was particularly distressing to see the children. In escaping from the Nazis, people abandoned everything, left their homes, sometimes only managing to grab a bit of food and clothing, sometimes with nothing at all, actually shoeless and half-dressed.

My cousin Nina Mikhailovna Datsenko (Uncle Misha's daughter), who lived in the Ukraine before the war, escaped the rapidly approaching Nazi forces, which brought destruction, violence, grief and tears, and fled in nothing more than a summer dress with no other personal effects. Along with a crowd of refugees she traversed many tens of kilometres on foot along the road east. Subsequently Nina fought under the command of Zygmunt Berling in the Polish Army in the USSR, formed in 1943, attaining the rank of junior lieutenant and gaining numerous Polish military decorations.

Uralsk was filling up with these unfortunate people, who had lost everything.

These days the generosity, kindness and consideration shown by people during the war years is rarely remembered – only on anniversaries. But if back then there had not been universal compassion for people in their plight, we might not have held out. How many children survived merely because many families fostered orphans who had lost their parents somewhere or been evacuated from areas of military action! During the Soviet period a lot was written about such cases. I recall one woman in Tashkent fostering sixteen children of different nationalities. That, of course, was an exceptional case, but many took one or two children. And although times were hard, they helped and supported those for whom life was worse, even more difficult, than their own.

The people of Uralsk shared everything they had with the refugees: the roofs over their heads, warmth, their meagre provisions, clothing, footwear. Bread was only available through ration cards – 800 grams per day for manual workers, and less for other employees and children: 400 and 600 grams. Butter, sugar and tea, which were also rationed, practically disappeared from our table. The collective farm market had everything. But whereas the state-controlled prices for bread and other foodstuffs remained unchanged throughout the war, they immediately increased sharply at the farm market and then continued to climb. Groceries were very dear. Thus, a kilogram of butter cost 1,000 rubles and a loaf of black bread – 200 (by comparison my pay at the factory was about 800–1,000 rubles per month).

These days, when prices go up week by week in peace-time conditions and many vitally important food items have become inaccessible, it is impossible even to imagine how the country's leadership managed to keep state prices unchanged for the four wartime years, when a significant part of the economy lay in ruins and the remainder was operating for the army and the front.

Time went by. The war rolled east and the Germans captured one town after another. The radio at home remained switched on day and night; everyone anxiously listened to the broadcasts from the Soviet bureau of information, nervous and agitated. We will probably never forget that round, black speaker hanging on the wall, which people gathered around to learn the latest news from the front.

But for us it was holiday time, and we were bored by the prospect of having nothing to do. Eventually our time came.

One day all Komsomol (Young Communist League) members – I had joined in March 1941 – were assembled at school and it was announced that we were going to a collective farm to work. By that time a great many young fit men had already been called up for military service, and those left in the villages were mainly women, old folk and children. But the people and the army had to be fed. The Germans had occupied a significant amount of territory in the European part of the country and therefore it was very important that the harvest should not be allowed to fail in the eastern regions. All this was explained to us. Harvesting began.

Yet it was an extraordinary time. I am always amazed when I look back and recall those events. All of us who had completed seven years of schooling were obliged to take part in a cross-country run within the framework of the 'Ready for Work and Defence' sporting programme. On the set day hardly anybody turned up; there was a war on, so what talk could there be of cross-country running! But when we were told that those who did not turn up would not be going to the collective farm, everyone came.

And so we arrived at the collective farm to work morning to evening in the fields under the baking sun. Everyone got sunburnt and their skin peeled off in clumps. There was nobody to cook for us because every pair of hands was needed in the fields. We did the cooking ourselves, taking turns. To call it cooking would be an exaggeration. We boiled stuff where we were, in the fields, on a camp fire, in a huge cauldron. I waited in dread for my turn to come, as I did not know how to cook at all. No miracle occurred and my turn to boil the porridge came. I can visualise it like yesterday: the camp fire, the cauldron black with soot, and the millet porridge boiling over the edge. I had put too much grain in and there was no room for it in the huge pot. There I stood in deep red, loose satin trousers, sunburnt and tearful – from the smoke, the pain of my scalded hands, and vexation at my ineptitude. And I was ashamed too; folk would arrive tired and hungry, and there would be . . . But they didn't say anything, ate up all the porridge, and licked their spoons. They were hungry all right! Alas, I was not the only bumbler. We had to eat similar 'culinary masterpieces' quite often.

I did not work till the end of summer. I caught scarlet fever and was taken back to Uralsk and put into hospital. I don't remember how long I lay there. Soon after discharge I fell ill again, with temperature fluctuations between 35 and 40 degrees Celsius and unbearable headaches, so much so that even my hair became a handicap, seemingly crushing my head like an iron band. I asked my father to shave it off. He didn't argue, took some electrical clippers and removed all my hair. For a long time, they were unable to make a diagnosis. One day on the street my mother met a doctor named Keller, who was well known in the city, one of the exiled Volga Germans. And even though he was off somewhere in a real hurry in his buggy, he agreed to take a look at me. He sounded my lungs, examined me and diagnosed typhoid fever. It was back to the hospital again. I remember the horror that gripped me when I ended up in the same ward where I had lain the first time and on the bed where the neighbouring patient at the time had died. 'That means I'm going to die too' – that was my first thought. I instantly lost consciousness for a long time. Everything else that occurred before my consciousness returned, I know only from what my mother told me. The situation was almost hopeless. I was unconscious for a very long time, my temperature was constantly around the 39–40-degree mark, and my heart struggled to cope. One day they actually let mum and dad in to say goodbye to me, even though the department was meant to be sterile and nobody was allowed near the patients. The doctor told them that everything depended on my heart – would it hold out or not. I can imagine their situation. Mum later told me that she came to the hospital every morning and fearfully looked in the window of my ward, which was on the ground floor. If my blanket from home was still visible, that meant I was still alive. And this went on for a number of weeks.

It was already winter when I came to. There were hard frosts. The heating in the hospital depended on furnaces, there was not enough firewood, and every day my parents brought a few logs to warm my ward up. I was not allowed to eat the coarse food and needed white bread, butter, and fruit juices. But where could they be obtained when there was a strict rationing system in operation and the prices at the market put everything out of reach? Only speculators could afford such luxury. Quite a few of them had started operating during the war. You could obtain foodstuffs in return for jewellery or high quality articles. But in our family, we had never had anything like that. My father found a solution; he gathered up all the more or less decent looking things we had (a carpet, his new woollen suit, some calfskin boots and other stuff) and set off around the villages. He came back with a sack of apples, a small amount of white flour, and a little bit of butter. Now almost every day mum or dad brought me white rusks, fruit juice and eggs. Little by little I began to get better.

One day there was a knock on the window during non-visiting hours. I looked out and saw under the window the joyful smile of my best friend, Lucia Malinovskaya. She was saying something and pointing at her head. I could not hear anything through the double glazing and did not understand what she wanted. Then Lucia took off her head-scarf and I saw that her skull was shaved! It turned out she had done this out of solidarity with me. What a crackpot!

It seems I spent three months lying in the hospital and left it in such a weak condition that I had to learn how to walk again, holding on to the head of a bed or the back of a chair. My head shaved, thin as a skeleton, and barely able to stand up, I experienced an acute sense of joy: I was still alive! I walked around the room, touching things, looked out the window and again experienced that same joy. Joy that I could walk, see, talk, listen.

Then I began to go outside. Then came the day when I decided to go to school, to see my classmates. We had a class renowned for its solidarity, I was greeted with rapture and, when Lucia Malinovskaya dashed over to hug me, I was barely able to stay on my feet from weakness, fell over and dragged her down after me. We both lay on the floor laughing out loud, and the whole class laughed along with us.

I was unable to return to school that year; I was hopelessly behind by half a year, and I did not have the strength to study.

When I began to go out again after I was well, it seemed to me that there were significantly more people in the town than there had been before I fell ill. Indeed, such was the case. Some factories and military colleges had been transferred to Uralsk from the west and refugees were constantly arriving. It all added up to more and more people.

During the war years the population of Uralsk increased by approximately 40,000 and reached the 100,000 mark. Later I found out that, at the decision of the Stalingrad Front military council, Uralsk had become part of the front zone and a centre of anti-aircraft defence.

CHAPTER 2

Everything for the Front

In 1942 our school was closed and a hospital located in its premises. Its pupils dispersed in various directions: some transferred to other schools, many in the senior classes went off to work, and others left town altogether.

I have to confess that at that time I was what is termed a 'mummy's girl': spoilt, timid, dependent on others, ill-adapted to face life's various difficulties and hassles. But the moment the question arose as to what I should do, I suddenly realised clearly that in this situation responsibility for my future could not be placed on somebody else's shoulders, that I must make my own decision. And I made it: I would go to work at a factory.

At the same time a summons had arrived for me: I was being mobilised for the labour front – for the time being, as an apprentice in the school of factory tuition. Yes, there was even mobilisation of labour during the war years. My mother went with me to the commission, presented a certificate that I had a heart defect, and I received a temporary extension until I was completely well. It was embarrassing to evade call-up, but for some reason I did not want to go to that school, and my mother's actions drew no protest from me. However, on leaving the school, I told Mum straight away that I could not lie around with nothing to do and I would go to a military factory. Mum objected because my heart really was bothering me a great deal after the typhoid attack, but my mother offered to arrange a job for me somewhere more restful, doing clerical work. And for the first time in my sixteen years I responded with a firm 'no', declared that I would only go to a military factory, and would acquire a working profession at all costs. All my relatives tried to dissuade me from what was in their view a rash step, but I insisted on my choice. And won out.

I went to defence factory no. 321, where I was assigned to workshop no. 8. The question of suitable clothing arose. Nothing appropriate could be found at home, so relatives came to the rescue. Aunt Lida (Mum's elder sister, Lida Ivanovna Sinodaltseva) brought along her old overcoat; it was a bit long, to be sure, and a bit voluminous but, girded by a belt, it would do. Somebody else gave me a silk shawl, which was white at the time of donation, but turned grey within a few days and never recovered its original colour, despite all our efforts. I also received some felt boots with leather patches on the backs of the heels, while other relations came up with a spare cap and some mittens.

I did not look very impressive, to put it mildly, but back then there were few at the factory who looked any better, and nobody paid attention. We had other problems.

My first work-day dawned. I presented my pass at the gateway, walked through the grounds, found my work section, presented my pass once again, and went in. Our section was situated amidst some former auto-repair workshops. What I saw here stunned me: a huge workshop, cold walls, concrete floor. Visible here and there were cast-iron furnaces, but they gave off little heat and it was so cold that you could see your own breath. The whole workshop was occupied by lathes: turning, milling, grinding, drilling, boring and others still. Some were huge and long, while others were small, table-size. They stood very close to one another; evidently the shop management had striven to fit as much equipment as possible into the allotted space. Everything was whirling, droning, graunching, squealing. The noise was unimaginable.

But the most striking impression was of the people working here. They were mainly women and teenagers – all in winter coats, wadded jackets or sheepskins, with winter caps or headscarves, and wearing felt boots. Despite the extreme cold, they all worked with their minds on the job. And how they worked! I noticed that some of the adolescents were standing on boxes. I thought this was for warmth, but then realised that many of them would not have been able to operate the lathes without these boxes. Unsurprisingly, some of the boys and girls were as young as thirteen or fourteen.

Working in our section was a remarkable lad named Kolya Gryekov. He had arrived at the factory as a sixteen-year-old and within a year he was heading a brigade of lathe operators and assemblers. Apart from him the brigade included four other workers – two of his own age, a third who had just turned fourteen, and another who was barely twelve. The brigade coped superbly with the heavy, labour-intensive work. In return for its fine performance, its young leader was given an award consisting of a cotton emblem to be attached to his clothing. This was typical for factories in those days.

I should mention that in 1943 the USSR Council of Ministers issued a decree providing for the organisation of evening schools in which young workers could receive secondary education at their workplace. These days this sounds amazing; there was a bloody war raging, everything took second place to the needs of the front, to the defeat of the enemy – and here they were setting up workers' schools. They were established all over the country, including in Uralsk. Many young workers from our factory entered this school, Kolya among them. It was very hard to combine work and study, but the factory management strove to provide at least the basic needs for teenagers engaged in study.

Whatever the difficulties created for production, on days when classes took place, the working day was shortened by two hours, and during exam time paid leave was granted. The school also provided food: a piece of bread and a cup of tea were offered on top of normal rations. Many people, if not everybody, managed to obtain a secondary education through that school. Kolya also completed his schooling successfully and after the war entered the Leningrad Polytechnic Institute. He subsequently spent the rest of his life working for the Electrosila plant, becoming the chief mechanic of the plant and then the entire chain. He wrote a thesis for his candidate of science degree and published two monographs.

Zhenya Korotin came to the factory when he was fifteen. He was appointed as a lathe repairman, even though up till then he had only ever seen them in the cinema or in pictures. But there was a shortage of specialists and even children were appointed to important areas. Zhenya proved to be a bright and meticulous lad, and responsible beyond his years; he soon mastered what was for him a new craft and quickly learned to fix all the lathes, restoring life even to the oldest ones, which graunched and rattled from age and overload. Everybody was certain that he would turn out to be a splendid engineer. But Zhenya became a doctor of philology, devoted his whole life to collecting the folklore of the Ural Cossacks, and published several books. He spent his last years in St Petersburg, but often visited Uralsk at the invitation of the local Cossacks, and they regarded him as a national hero.

Victoria Yakusheva and I had known each other since the days when we attended the same nursery school. At the beginning of the war she also came to our factory, worked as a turner – not in our workshop but in the 9th one. After the war Victoria went on to higher education, wrote a dissertation for a candidate's degree and taught for many years in the Uralsk institute of education.

I could tell a number of other similar stories about those who worked at our factory during the war years. Information about some of them has been assembled in the factory museum, which was set up after the war, and also in the Uralsk Museum named in honour of Hero of the Soviet Union Manshuk Mamyetova, a native of our city who volunteered for the front and lost her life in combat. And on the factory grounds a monument was erected in honour of Pyotr Alexandrovich Atoyan, who literally set up the factory on an empty site and then ran it continuously for over forty years. Fresh flowers are to be seen there at any time of the year.

When I recall our workshop, I can still visualise to this day the long cigar-shaped bodies of the torpedoes, polished till they gleamed, and the huge circular nautical mines. And the people – dead tired from overwork and lack of sleep, emaciated, ever hungry, blue with cold. Over the war period the factory supplied the ships of our navy with around 4,000 mines of various kinds. Practically every twentieth enemy ship was blown up by a mine manufactured at our factory. And it is no secret that the gigantic German passenger liners *Wilhelm Gustloff* and *General von Steuben*, both of which had been pressed into service as armed transports, were sunk early in 1945 by torpedoes from our factory.

When I started work, I found out that there were only a few men in the workshop, among them team leader Ivanov and instrument-maker Poltyev. It was the latter I reported to. He was a vile old man, a real grubber, always seeking to grab more for himself, even falsifying requests on official forms. But he was an ace in his own field and indeed the only specialist of his kind. So we put up with him.

I was appointed to the instrument storeroom and at the same time Poltyev was charged with teaching me what he did. And what he did was highly responsible work – assembling some parts of the fuzes in sea-mines and torpedoes. Many items were made by hand. I no longer remember the names of these articles and their components, but the main point was that without them not even a single shell would have detonated.

My supervisor's workplace was set up in the same place, in the storeroom where I worked. This enabled me to use every minute free from my basic job to good advantage, learning Poltyev's skills. True, there were few spare minutes at first. But later, when I had become accustomed to the work and begun to cope better with the duties of a storeman, the tuition went more rapidly.

It was hard work, spending the whole day on your feet. I would issue the instruments and check them in again: hand-drills, hacksaws, hammers, chisels, drill bits, milling cutters, punches, etc. It's easy to say, that I gave them out and checked them back in again. Every item had to be put back on the rack in the right spot. The spaces for them had to be clearly distinguished; for instance, a drill bit of one diameter could not be put in with those of a different diameter, or else it would never be found again. And there was a queue at the issue hatch; everyone was in a hurry for the tools, so as not to waste time. And it was like that from morning to evening, for twelve hours (such was the length of the working day).

How many tears I shed! There was a catastrophic shortage of instruments as it was. And the boys often spoiled them, broke them, sometimes owing to inexperience, but sometimes from playing around – they were after all still children. And the workers were demanding, shouting, cursing. All day the sound was in my ears: 'Come on, quickly!' You would approach the instrument-sharpener with a broken or blunt tool and he would also get abusive and shout: 'How did you let the instrument get into such a bad state? Sharpen it yourself!' But how could I sharpen it if I didn't know how? Thank heaven for my instructor; although he wasn't much of a man, he was a human being, though he still needled me. Sometimes he would sharpen the instrument himself, but the main thing was that he taught me how to do it. Things got a lot better.

Subsequently I was admitted to the factory's real work; along with my elderly instructor I began to assemble those very items on which the entire team was reliant. The amount of production from the workshop depended on the number we both put together. I soon gained the professional grading of instrument-turner, third class.

As for the instruments, another girl had to weep over them. True, it was easier for her; I helped her a little when I could.

Working at the factory, we keenly felt (and I really mean 'felt') the situation in the naval battle zones. There were days, and quite often, when the entire workshop team was assembled for a five-minute meeting and told that we had to put in extra hours. We realised that either there were fierce battles at sea somewhere, or major naval operations were being planned, and extra production would be required of us. Overtime work might go on for a day and a night, or even two or three days and nights. We spent the nights in the workshop. We would bed down on benches, on boxes, or by the lathes. On these days we were given extra rations in the factory cafeteria.

Sometimes people would drop off to sleep right at their work-places. This led to all sorts of mishaps, including injuries and mutilations. After an accident, casualties were sent home for twelve hours to rest, and then it was back to work.

But nobody grumbled. 'Everything for the front! Everything for victory!' – these words became the country's main slogan during the four long years of the war. People toiled hugely and self-sacrificingly, struggling to over-fulfil the plan. The best brigades were awarded the title 'Front-Line Brigade'. And how many voluntary donations there were to the defence fund for the construction of tanks and aircraft! People handed in their jewellery, money, antiques. Women, both old and young, knitted socks and mittens for the soldiers, and sometimes gave their last coins to buy them tobacco and cigarettes, and all this was sent to the front. They wrote letters to the soldiers. There were numerous blood donors during those years; people gave blood to save the lives of the wounded.

At military factories, and in other organisations too, discipline was strict. In accordance with the wartime laws absenteeism, infractions of discipline, and damage to production were harshly punished, even to the extent of criminal charges being pressed. A fourteen-year-old boy, who worked at the same factory as I did, missed a couple of days for some reason and was sentenced to a year of corrective labour in a penal colony for juvenile law-breakers. But without strict discipline we would not have been able to achieve what we did. In the case of our factory, the equipment had not been completely installed before the workers began delivering output on the lathes that had been set up. It was like that everywhere. In some places it was done differently: lathes would be set up under the open sky, work would begin to fulfil military orders, and parallel with this the walls would be built around them and the roof put on – that was how new factories for the production of military technology and weapons were established. Without strict discipline, order, and organisation it would have been impossible.

Working habits did not come easily to me. At that time, I did not know how to do anything. My parents had not even taught me to do housework. I think one reason for this was my constant illness. I went down with practically all the children's ailments, and then had scarlet fever and typhoid, so naturally my health was not the best. And my parents protected me.

The factory certainly left its mark on me. How many times I damaged my fingers with a hammer, and scraped them with a whetstone. The dirt would get into the wounds and everything would begin to fester and swell. I remember getting up in the morning with fingers like sausages. I would knead them, rub them, squeeze the pus out where possible and go to work. More than anything at that time I dreamt of being able to work in gloves. But, alas, only those who worked with large items or engaged in welding were allowed to do this. The articles we worked with were very small; sometimes you could barely pick them up with your bare hands. And it was so cold that your skin sometimes froze to the metal and then peeled off in strips.

I was perpetually hungry, and I wasn't the only one. Although I received 800 grams of bread a day in accordance with the worker's ration, what sort of bread was it? You could squeeze a piece of it in your fist, then unfold your fingers, and the bread would remain a dark grey compressed lump. But there was nothing else to take to work with you. And bread like this was not filling. True, sometimes we got a bite to eat in the factory cafeteria, but that was irregular. We were also poorly nourished at home.

At one time things got really bad. Then my father put his last pair of calf-skin boots, a lovely winter jacket, and other stuff into a sack, went out to the countryside again, and exchanged it all for a sack of flour made from millet husks. We were overjoyed: a whole sack of flour, not real flour, but you could cook flat cakes and pancakes with it. Alas, our joy proved premature: the flour turned out to be very bitter, with a taste like quinine. I don't know whether it had spoiled in the home of the sellers or was naturally like that, because I have never tasted anything like it since. But we still made flat cakes out of it – without yeast, without salt, without oil – simply mixed them with water and placed the fry-pan containing this wartime culinary masterpiece in a Russian stove. And ate them. I recall putting a piece in my mouth and wondering whether to swallow it or spit it out. We swallowed it nevertheless; hunger got the better of us. The bitter taste would remain in your mouth for a long time afterwards.

But there were some truly wonderful days in our life. In honour of some anniversary my father was once issued special rations as a participant in the October Revolution. What it was about I don't remember. When I went into the room and looked at the table, the sight of a hunk of real soft, spongy, white bread with a fragrant crust leapt out at me. This loaf of wheaten bread, which was so unusual for that time, literally bewitched me. I carefully took it in my hands and sliced it right on my palm, so that no crumb would go to waste. The knife turned out to be serrated, and I cut my hand, but I could not waste a crumb, so I ate it along with the droplets of blood. To this day I can still visualise that slab of magnificent bread.

Another time my mother was given a whole pot of greasy meat stock. We put it outside in the frost. Then we skimmed off the congealed fat, fried something in it, and made soup for several days from the diluted, fat-free bouillon. It was hard to call it soup; it contained some sort of grain and a little salt. But it was still broth from meat stock.

During the war the most dependable form of currency was vodka; you could exchange it for anything. For half a litre of vodka at the market, for example, they would give you half a kilo of butter. My father once got hold of three bottles of vodka, which we put in a safe place. At that time an old woman used to call on us from time to time. She was lonely, eternally hungry, but always clean, tidy (how she managed that in the absence of soap and suchlike, I do not understand), and extraordinarily obliging. We called her Auntie Tanya. I don't recall where she came from, but we were very fond of her, gave her a little extra food when we had any, and she would help mum around the house. We all worked from early morning to late at night and there was simply no time for domestic chores. And Auntie Tanya felt better when she was helping us. 'At least I'm earning my keep,' she would say, when some job was found for her.

One day she took it upon herself to wash the floor, accidentally bumped one of the vodka bottles, which fell over and knocked the others over. All three were smashed! For us it was a very palpable loss and we were terribly upset. Nobody said anything to Auntie Tanya, but for a very long time she felt that she was to blame. Whenever she came, she would weep: 'What have I done, old fool that I am!' We comforted her as best we could.

At the factory everything went on as normal. I was elected a member of the Young Communist League committee. My main obligation was looking after pupils at the factory school, which trained workers for the factory – the same school I had recently been called up for and had no wish to attend.

I was already seventeen years old, but not renowned for my vigour and independence, and was not always able to stand up for myself. But now I had to defend the interests of several dozen teenagers, to ensure that their practical production work proceeded in an organised way, and day to day needs and rations were provided for. My position made this obligatory. I gradually learned to argue with management, prove my point, get what I wanted, and now and then things began to work out well. At any rate that was how my work was evaluated by our factory newspaper, which I have kept.

All in all, there was plenty to do; I was essentially occupied with both factory and community matters, and there wasn't time to be bored.

But youth is youth. Whenever there was free time (true, it did not occur that often), I met with my earlier friends, went visiting, or to the cinema, or even to dances.

One day I learnt that my classmate Volodya Chemryaiev had ended up in the hospital located at our school. With my mother's permission I spent part of my wages, bought something tasty at the market, and set off to visit the wounded casualty. We talked for a long time. Volodya said that at sixteen years old he had outwitted all the commissions and managed to get into military college, while at seventeen he became a company commander, got wounded and was now being treated within the walls of his old school. As we bade farewell, Volodya said: 'You know, Yulia, I'm being sent to the Stalingrad front and I've got a feeling I won't come back from there.' And so it turned out; he lost his life at Stalingrad. Another classmate, Yury Zaitsev, also volunteered for the front. He survived but lost an arm.

With regard to the other boys in my pre-war class I know nothing. All in all, my contemporaries, born in the year 1926, were lucky; many of them were not even called up into the army and remained alive.

It was already 1943. Summer had arrived and things had become a little easier. Everyone felt a bit livelier, got a new lease on life, as they say. We went out picking berries, gathered mushrooms, caught fish. Our area had lots of rivers. Apart from the Ural river, there was the Chagan, which flowed along the edge of the city, the Derkul, and other streams. There were plenty of fish in them at that time, and in the Ural, there were even sturgeon. So, we never came back from fishing empty-handed. My mother was given a tiny allotment outside the city, where we planted potatoes and, in the autumn, we took in a fairly good harvest. It never ceases to amaze me that, although this was a time of extreme hunger, nobody stole potatoes from our allotment.

Generally speaking the food situation got a little better in 1943. My friend from the factory Yulia Largina recalled that, when we worked the night shift together, mum would make us potato salad for our dinner break (at midnight). We used to go back to my place (the factory was a ten-to-fifteen-minute walk). 'We would eat a whole bowl full of potato salad,' Yulia recalled. 'Down to the last speck.'

As time went by, I grew well accustomed to the work, became a real worker. However, the idea of going to the front never left me.

Then, one morning on the street, I met Valya Shilova, a friend since nursery school days. True, she was two years older than me, so we were in different groups at nursery and in different classes at school. We ended up at the same factory in different workshops. We became friends thanks to our mothers, who had been in the same Young Communist League branch when they were young and had remained friends during the intervening years.

Valya was an extraordinary person. One rarely encounters such kind folk, who are responsive to others' joys and woes and incapable by nature of dishonesty and deception even in the smallest degree. Although frail and short of stature, she was strong and determined nevertheless and this became particularly manifest during her army service. I was struck most of all by her eyes, which were bright, clear, and somehow of extraordinary depth. Somebody told me once that people with eyes like that don't live long. Unfortunately, this prophecy came true; she lost her life three months later at the front.

When I met Valya that summer morning, I found out that two-week courses in basic military training for girls, away from the workplace, had been organised in the city. Acceptance depended on the recommendation of one's Young Communist League branch. Valya had already joined up. 'Enough,' I said, 'my time has come. I'm going to attend these courses as well.' Valya tried to cool my ardour, telling me that girls were not accepted below the age of eighteen. I was half a year away from my eighteenth birthday, but I resolved to join this course whatever it took; it meant there was a real chance of getting closer to my dream of reaching the front.

The first day of training arrived. I was supposed to take my passport, but I naturally turned up without any documents. In reply to a question about my passport I responded with some incomprehensible drivel. The first time they believed me, but when it was repeated on the second and the third day, the instructors of course cottoned on that I did not yet have one. However, for some reason I was not excluded from the group. Possibly they were taken in by my passionate desire to get to the front and the zeal with which I approached the training, but maybe the required recruiting target had not been met. I don't know. The training load on the course was very heavy; we were involved for seven or eight hours every day, including weekends and public holidays. We were taught the military code, basic parade-ground drill, crawling on our elbows, camouflage, trench-digging and even small-bore rifle shooting – and all outside, whatever the weather. So far as I recall, not one of the girls flinched despite the difficulties. After two weeks certificates were issued to testify completion of tuition on an elementary military training course. Once again, they asked to see my passport. Alas, I was not yet eighteen years old, so I had no passport to show; thus, I was the only one in the group not to receive a certificate. At the time I did not attach any significance to it; it was just a bit of paper, after all.

Half a year went by. Then one day, when I was on my way to work, I bumped into Valya by the factory entrance (one of life's coincidences). She was looking very tense. I was surprised; our shift was about to start and she was leaving the factory. It turned out that Valya and other girls who had completed the same course which I had attended on a legally dubious basis had received call-up papers from the enlistment office. And this was based on the very course certificates which I had so contemptuously dismissed. I did not go to work and decided to accompany Valya to the enlistment office, even though I would be threatened with serious punishment for unauthorised absence from work and could end up in court. But at that moment I didn't even consider that. I had to get to the front!

When we arrived at the enlistment office, all the girls from the course were gathered there. They began to produce their documents, including the unfortunate certificates. It was only then that I realised that I had no documents with me except my factory pass. I did not give up, but went with the others into the office of the city military commissar, who received us personally for some reason, probably because the recruits were somewhat out of the ordinary. I sat on the most distant chair, nearest the door, and began to wonder how to get myself out of this plight. I couldn't think of anything. But on learning that I had no documents at all, the commissar refused even to talk to me and suggested I return to the factory and work for the front. With some difficulty I persuaded him to listen to me. He did so, was surprised that I had completed the course with maximum marks, but refused to arrange call-up documents. As I left, he asked if I was the daughter of Alexander Ivanovich Zhukov.

From the enlistment office I went back to the factory but work did not go well. My thoughts were occupied by one thing: how to get to the front with the other girls. I returned home after the shift around midnight. My mother was still awake. She was upset for some reason and standing by a basin savagely pummelling some washing.

'What's the matter, mum? Are you upset?'

'Do you think I ought to be pleased at you going to the enlistment office without telling your father and me and asking to be sent to the front? You're still a girl; you've got a bad heart. They're still not even calling up lads of your age.'

'But I'm a Young Communist League member, mum, and I've done that special course.'

All in all, it proved a difficult conversation. At the time I was unable to work out how my mother had found out about my visit to the enlistment office; I assumed that one of the girls had blurted it out. Distressed by the conversation with my mother, I went to bed without realising that my parents would not sleep at all that night, wondering what they should do.

It was only after the war that mum told me that the city military commissar, who knew her well, had telephoned her straight after I had left, told her everything and promised to do what she decided. It was not difficult to imagine what state my mother was in, and my father as well. They told me nothing about the phone call and did not sleep all night, wondering, debating how they should act. Giving their consent would be a frightening decision; I could be killed or spend my whole life as an invalid. No less difficult for them was the alternative: not to let me go to the front. They were worried as to how I would feel and how I would relate to them if I found out sometime that they had used their official position and authority to close down my ambitions. All in all, there were many questions, but only two answers: yes or no. After an arduous, sleepless night Mum rang the commissar and said 'Yes'.

After the war I was told that one day in conversation with someone my mother had dropped the phrase: 'If anything happens, Yulia will never forgive us for not letting her go to the front.' I don't know what she meant; I never talked to her about it.

And so, my parents took what for them was a very hard decision. It was not made easily and demanded real courage on their part. After all, I hadn't quite turned eighteen, my health was not very good, and I was their only child. Perhaps some would have condemned them, but I am grateful to my parents for overcoming their fears and doubts and taking that decision. If things had been otherwise, I could possibly have remained my whole life the way I was: shy, timid, and lacking in self-confidence. The army and the front radically changed me, my character, indeed, my whole life. Not only did I begin to take a different attitude to the world around me, but the attitudes of others towards me changed.

The main thing was that I lived during the post-war years with a sense of personal participation in our great victory, with a feeling of pride that during my country's dark days I was not left sitting on the side-line. It is a source of great happiness when you have something to be proud of.

There is one more thing I can say with complete certainty: at a later stage I was constantly depressed by a feeling of guilt that I had sat it out in the rear for a time and thus remained alive, while my friend Valya Shilova went to the front and lost her life. For many years after the war I felt myself to blame for the fact that during secondment at sniper school I showed no initiative and did nothing to get into the same military unit as Valya. It is possible that everything would have been different. But perhaps that is the way fate decided, for there was always something keeping us apart. At military school we ended up in different companies and we were assigned to different fronts.

But before departure one further event occurred that was important for me. Since birth I had been called Yulia Valeryanovna Alexeyeva, after the name of my real father. When my mother married for the second time, she retained her maiden name, Sinodaltseva, as she had done in the case of her first marriage. Our family looked a little odd in this respect: my (step-)father was Zhukov, my mother Sinodaltseva, and my surname was Alexeyeva. Later on, when my step-father was released from imprisonment, mum took his name, while I remained with my own. My father, and I always called him that, raised the question of changing my name several times with mum, but for some reason she would not agree. And now, with the last opportunity for legal adoption imminent (it was permitted only up to the age of eighteen), my father raised the question again. Mum agreed, but because I was already virtually an adult, the issue was handed over to me to decide. I loved my father, placed a high value on his attitude towards me, and therefore I could not fail to agree. He was pleased. Thus, I left work at the factory as Alexeyeva, and set off for military school as Zhukova.

CHAPTER 3

My Family's Tragedy

Working on my memoirs of late I have been thinking more and more often about my parents. I remember my dear, affectionate, mother, who was always not just a mother to me but a real friend. I recall my outwardly stern, but very kind and considerate father. I gaze into the past and somehow experience anew those years gone by, find myself again and again thinking how much my parents had to endure, how many days of grief fell to their lot, including those on my account. First, my endless childhood illnesses. Then the typhoid and constant anxiety: would I survive or not? Then the factory, where I had to work for days on end, cold and hungry, with a weak heart to boot, while my parents worried about me and my health. And then the front, and again my parents' life was filled with anxiety and tension: would I return or not? Would I be wounded or not? In 1948 I left for Moscow, where I studied at first and then remained to work. Eleven months in Moscow and just one at home with my parents. And once again they lived in expectation, awaiting my letters, my holidays or periods of leave, and my visits . . .

I realise that this is the fate of all parents. But this fact does not make it any easier for anyone. There was some comfort for them: I never took my obligations as a daughter lightly. I loved my mother and father and was never untrue to them in thought or deed. Even when my father was arrested as an 'enemy of the people', I firmly declared: 'I don't believe that my father is an enemy of the people.' I was only thirteen, but I was convinced of his innocence.

It happened in March 1939. Eighty years have passed since that time. The 1930s were a tragic period for our country. Many innocent people were subjected to repression and hundreds of thousands were shot. Misfortune touched our family too.

That year we lived in Barnaul. My father worked as a section head in the regional branch of the NKVD (the National Commissariat for Internal Affairs). I don't remember what title he bore; in photographs he wore two squares on his tabs. He was undoubtedly a person of some merit. Mum worked in the same branch, held a low rank, but did very important work – coding and decoding.

We lived in a large brick house with four rooms, fitted out with government-issue furniture and an inventory number on every item. There was no point in accumulating furniture because Dad was often transferred from city to city and, when we moved house, we took only our personal things. Dad was provided with accommodation from work, and in each new place our apartment was again fitted out with furniture bearing inventory numbers. As a result of frequent moves, by the time I was in the fifth grade, I had already changed schools several times between Alma-Ata, (now Almaty, Kazakhstan), Novosibirsk and Barnaul.

At home I had my own room. I could walk into the house, take the corridor to the right and there was my abode, where I slept, did homework and played.

On that day in March 1939 I came home from school and, as usual, headed straight for my room. At first, I did not even notice the wax seal on the door. I only saw it when I tried to enter. The door was locked and on it hung a large red wax seal. I rushed over to see Marfa Ivanovna, our domestic help, and it was then that I saw there were a lot of military people in the house. I was escorted into the living room. Here a search was nearing completion. There were various articles, books and papers lying scattered around the floor; drawers had been removed, and their contents tossed out indiscriminately. It looked as if everything had been turned upside down. On the divan sat my mother, motionless, with a white frozen face. She was not crying. I sat down beside her and asked what had happened, and was told: 'Your father has been arrested as an enemy of the people.' My reaction was instant: 'No! I don't believe dad is an enemy of the people.'

Dad had been arrested at work. Mum was also dismissed and expelled from the Party as the wife of an 'enemy of the people'.

Later, when my father returned, mum would tell him of my reaction to his arrest. And he would say to me literally with tears in his eyes: 'I will never forget this. Thank you, girl.'

However, that would be almost a year later. That day the men in uniform completed their search, collected documents, dad's decorations, and a whole heap of photographs, and left, telling us on their way out to vacate the house within a day.

Mum found a tiny room somewhere, eight or nine square metres in area. Taking our clothes and my textbooks and toys, which I was unwilling to part with for anything, we moved into the new place the following day.

Mum and I remained completely devoid of any means of subsistence, because my parents were never able to save money, while employment exit payments were naturally not made in such cases. Mum tried to inquire about her husband, visited some offices, wrote to others, but without result. We had no relations in Barnaul, friends and acquaintances were afraid to socialise with us and, if they met you on the street, they would hurriedly cross to the other side or turn away, pretending that they did not know us.

At first I would tell my mother: 'They haven't noticed us. Let's call out to them.' Mum would usually remain silent. But one day she stopped, turned me towards her and said: 'Yulia, you're a big girl now and you must realise: we are now the family of an enemy of the people. Folk are afraid to have anything to do with us.' I did not understand anything and thought to myself: if it is clear to me that dad is not any enemy of the people, why do adults not realise that? And why are mum and I enemies of the people? Why are they afraid of us? But from then on, I stopped asking my mother about anything,

I stopped going to school; I was frightened and ashamed, and feared that they would question me or say something about it. One day we had a visit from our class teacher, Anna Alexandrovna Chebyshova. Her husband also worked for the NKVD, but she was not afraid; she came and had a long talk with mum. And then my classmates arrived, almost half of them. I had nowhere to invite them in, and we stood outside for a long time talking. Only much later did I realise that Anna Alexandrovna had officially committed a 'misdemeanour' by doing this.

Having failed to get anywhere with her inquiries, mum decided that we should go to our relatives in Uralsk. We travelled in a non-sleeper carriage. It was a long, long journey and for some reason our route took us through Moscow. I fell ill on the way. Mum was nervous, not knowing how we would be greeted in Uralsk. There were so many cases when wives renounced their husbands and children their parents in similar situations, when they were afraid to harbour relatives of somebody who had been arrested. And we were coming without warning . . .

We arrived at the home of mum's elder brother, Uncle Misha. Fortunately, both he and his wife greeted us with sympathy and understanding; they gave us warmth and succour and allotted us a room. Mum remained unemployed for a long time; nobody would take her on. Then somebody came to her assistance and she was hired as a laboratory assistant at a technical college. The pay was low, but it was something.

Time went by. Mum started writing away somewhere again, but in vain. She did not share her pain and anxiety with me, shielding me from needless worry. Then suddenly she left for Moscow without explaining anything to me. Only later, when she returned from Moscow, did I learn that she had been 'to see Stalin, to intervene for dad'. Did she realise what risk she was running? She could have been arrested as well. I think she did realise, but still went anyway! And a miracle occurred. The letter was delivered to Stalin and he ordered that my father's case should be carefully scrutinised again.

In memoirs from those years one can often read that many of those arrested and members of their families attempted to knock on Stalin's door, but that was useless and sometimes even dangerous. What prompted Stalin to give my father's case his attention? Were mum's arguments convincing? Or was he simply in a good mood? Or did he feel like creating a precedent? Or maybe we are obliged to whoever reported the matter to Stalin? Nobody knows. But my father's case was re-examined. Nobody could come up with any facts as to his 'hostile activity' and he was able to refute convincingly the trumped-up charges somebody had devised. He had not signed a single accusatory document in spite of beatings and threats. Father was released before the trial, so he did not have the threat of a court hearing hanging over him subsequently. Not so long ago I learned that dad was accused by his direct superior, to whom he was attempting to prove that there were not as many underground sabotage organisations in the city as the other imagined.

At the beginning of 1940 my father arrived back in Uralsk, thin, unshaven, in wadded prison garb, a grey convict's winter cap, and worn artificial leather boots – that was how he turned up.

His Party membership was restored and his decorations, documents and photographs were returned to him. Immediately after release in Barnaul he received an offer to go back to his previous job, but he refused and came to join us. A similar offer was then made to him in Uralsk, but he turned this down as well. He no longer wanted to work for the NKVD. He took on a job in economic management – as director of the city department for supplying the population with fuel. He remained in this position practically up to his death in 1959. He was highly appreciated at work and many in the city knew him and respected him for his exceptional honesty, decency, and eternal readiness to help people. He was one of those of whom it is said in Russia: 'He would give you his last shirt'. My father was a strong person, but his arrest broke him: he began to fall ill and died from heart failure at fifty-eight, outliving mum by one year and two months. I think it was because of the many ordeals she had to endure that my mother died so young (at the age of fifty-three).

My father did not like to talk about his arrest and the repressions of the 1930s in general. He most probably discussed it with mum, but not with me. Only once, soon after his return from confinement, he told me: 'Yulia, neither the Party nor Soviet power is responsible for what happened to me; the blame rests with particular people.' He did not name those people. There was also an instance when he related how he had been beaten by a young officer who had previously been his subordinate. He was beaten on the head with a stool, and began to cry. There were no further conversations on these topics.

In spite of all that, father remained a dedicated Communist and patriot to the end of his life. When the war began, he immediately went to the enlistment office, as I have described, to register as a volunteer; as an active participant in the October Revolution and a member of the Red Guards, he felt that he was obliged to be on the front line. Left behind in the rear, he did everything to help the families of front-line soldiers, especially of those who had lost their lives. Such was my step-father; I genuinely loved him, regarded him as a good father, and always called him 'dad'.

My mother's Party membership was also restored. Everything was eventually sorted out with regard to her employment and she was offered a job with the city Party committee.

Mum was very tender and kind, but highly principled when it came to serious matters. The saga with my father showed that she was also a very courageous and determined person. Risking not only her own life, but mine as well and my future, she rushed to the defence of her husband, for she was convinced of his complete innocence. Most people in this situation would have let it go, but she was not afraid. And she won through. It was just a pity that, all in all, her life turned out to be so tragic.

Many of those whose parents or other relatives were arrested relate that right throughout their entire subsequent life they lived in fear, felt some sort of trauma. That never happened to me – neither when my father was under investigation, nor later. I think it was due to the fact that my father was released quite quickly and was completely exonerated. Besides that, my parents always behaved with dignity wherever they were, giving nobody any pretext or opportunity to accuse them of anything.

My mother and father were well known in the city, enjoyed the respect of all who worked with them and also of many of those who appealed to them, even on just a single occasion, over some matter or other. They were both true Communists – dedicated, unbiased and honest.

They both grew up in ordinary families.

My mother, Alexandra Ivanovna Zhukova (née Sinodaltseva) was born on 7 July 1904, in Uralsk. Hers was a large family, eleven children in all. Some of them died in infancy and Uncle Volodya lost his life in the First World War. I knew three of mum's sisters and three of her brothers. The family did not have enough to live on and was unable to provide the children with a good education. Only the eldest brother, Uncle Misha, who suffered from severe heart disease, gained higher education and became a teacher; the others worked to support both him and the family. The children of mum's sisters and brothers knew no such problems. Born and growing up in the Soviet era, they all received higher education. My mother started work at sixteen – initially as a courier for the Cheka,* and then she trained as a coder and continued working with the security services until 1939 and the arrest of her second husband, my step-father. The last eight to ten years of her working life were spent with the Uralsk City Party committee as an instructor and assistant to the first secretary (quite a high-ranking position in Uralsk). The committee staff were fond of her and highly respected her. When she died (in 1957) they told me: 'We feel like orphans.' I was in such a state of despair myself that I thought I would never survive this loss. For me my mother embodied the very best, the very dearest qualities. It took me a long time to come to myself after this grief.

I have no memory of my natural father, Valeryan Alexandrovich Alexeyev; he left the family when I was still quite small. I don't know the reasons for the divorce, never asked my mother, and she did not talk about it. He died early, at the age of thirty or thirty-one, from heart failure at his workplace. He also worked for the security services, but in a different city.

My mother married for the second time when I was eight years old. My step-father, Konstantin Sergeyevich Zhukov, was born on 4 April 1900, in Moscow, in a working-class family. They lived in barracks – he, his elder sister and his father and mother. After completing four classes at school, at the age of twelve, he also started work at a factory. He was unable to continue his education, even though he was without question a talented individual. Everything that dad achieved in life was the result of huge exertion and constant, persistent self-education. Dad

---

* The Cheka, the first Soviet secret-police organisation, was established in December 1917 but replaced in 1922 by the OGPU.

was not even seventeen years old when he became a member of the Bolshevik Party. He took part in the October fighting in Moscow. When the Cheka was set up in 1919, he was assigned to work there. As a very young Cheka officer in 1924, he was one of the first to be awarded a distinguished Cheka badge (no. 106) and a certificate personally signed by Felix Dzerzhinsky. In the same year he was presented with the Order of the Red Banner. In subsequent years my father was twice rewarded with presentation weapons, which were confiscated during his arrest and never returned. I have as mementos some silver discs which were attached to the weapons upon presentation as confirmation that the recipient was being rewarded for specific services. Father worked in the security services for twenty years, right up to his arrest in 1939.

On his final journey to his resting place he was accompanied by hundreds of city residents who knew him as a man who was exceptionally sensitive and attentive to the needs of the people. A born and bred Muscovite, dad was buried in Uralsk, while mum, who was born in Uralsk and lived most of her life there, lies in the St Daniel Cemetery in Moscow. Such was their fate.

Our family had indeed suffered a grave tragedy. But nobody was bitter about it; nobody ever attempted to find those guilty for the misfortune which overtook us. It was impossible to set things straight again, but it was equally impossible to continue recalling those tragic events. Therefore, my parents avoided talking about that topic, as if excising from their lives what happened in 1939. I think that was wise.

I realise that that attitude is not to everyone's taste. However, those were the rules our family lived by. That is probably why I have never suffered from any complexes bound up with my father's arrest, unlike other people. I was not tormented by such humiliating emotions as fear, resentment and suspicion. My parents managed to protect me from all that.

The question of the repressions has been one of the most acute and painful issues in our society for many years. It seems to me that is impossible to speculate any further on this topic, to view it from a purely emotional stance, and to make wild estimates about the number of people who suffered, as is happening at the moment. You look at the figures which appear from time to time in the press and you wonder: who was it who fought at the front, who rebuilt the country after the war? It is time, I think, to conduct some serious investigation into this issue, so that specialists can establish the truth to the greatest possible extent and provide society with reliable information, however bitter its taste. Otherwise the passions raging in society will never die down.

CHAPTER 4

An Unusual Friendship

Before departing for the front, we had to face a medical commission. True, we were told it was just a formality, that almost everyone was passed fit, except that some would be approved for combatant and others for non-combatant service. I was nevertheless very nervous; a heart defect is no trifle. And what if I were passed fit for non-combatant service? In a laundry or kitchen, or as a cleaner, or in some hospital? All these were important of course, but I only wanted to be in a fighting unit and only at the front.

Now for the commission. We all knew that it was the physician who would have the decisive say, and therefore we were not afraid of the other doctors. I calmly went round the lot of them and approached the physician. And of all the luck! She turned out to be the doctor whose ward I had lain in with typhoid in 1941! As long as she didn't remember and recognise me! As if on purpose, she looked closely at me and said that my face was familiar. I fervently assured her that we simply could not have met anywhere, that I did not know her.

All in all, everything turned out well, but my nerves took a beating. It occurred to me that, if I had not changed my former name to that of my step-father by then, the doctor might have been able to recall the girl who seemed to be dying of typhoid in her ward.

And so the necessary documents were made out. Only now, with the decision of the medical commission in my hands, did I feel assured that my dream had become reality. Preparations for departure began.

Today, as I write this book, ever new events, facts and names surface in my memory. I sometimes wonder at this characteristic of the human memory – to be able to preserve the richest store of information for many long years and then release it at the required moment. As for my final days at home, they have been completely forgotten. Despite all my efforts, I cannot remember anything. It's a complete blank, a black hole, as if somebody has deliberately erased from my memory everything that happened during those days. No doubt, they were very sad days.

The day of departure arrived. I bade farewell to my home town, parents and friends. But before parting with everything that was so dear to me, I want to write about Taisia Valeryanovna Kulchitskaya, a remarkable person, fine actress, and a good and true friend of mine. I dedicate this chapter to her and our unusual friendship.

We met in 1943, when the operetta theatre in Petrozavodsk, in the Karelian–Finnish Soviet Autonomous Republic, was evacuated to Uralsk. Kulchitskaya was member of this theatre.

A very nice drama theatre had been built in Uralsk shortly before the war, but it had not managed to assemble a troupe of performers of its own. The theatre building of course did not lie idle, and staged various celebratory and festive events, Party and Young Communist League conferences, concerts and rallies. Sometimes it was used by second-rate drama groups or concert parties on tour, often of little interest. With the start of the war even these tours ceased and theatrical and concert life died.

Then suddenly our small city became the venue for a highly professional theatre with a magnificent troupe of performers, including several who bore the title 'Meritorious Artist' of their

Soviet republic. Our eyes leapt out of their sockets at the sight of the repertoire: *Silva, Countess Maritza, The Merry Widow, The Circus Princess, Die Fledermaus, Free Wind . . .*

The theatre immediately became the centre of unprecedented local commotion. Despite our lives of drudgery, everyone wanted to go to the theatre. Mum and I couldn't wait to get into some show either, never mind which one. My mother was unfamiliar with operetta as a theatrical genre, and I was even less accustomed to it, but it was a long time since we had seen good theatre at all. We chose to go to *Countess Maritza.*

So, there we were in the theatre. For me it was an unforgettable evening: Kalman's amazing music, young and handsome actors, excellent voices, a general atmosphere of festivity – it was all a real sensation.

The main roles that evening were played by Kulchitskaya and Nikolai Ruban – one of the theatre's two leading duos. They were both imposing in appearance, had strong, pure voices, and made a good artistic impression. The pair possessed an unusual charm. Apart from that, it seemed that they were made for each other, that this was a duo that simply could not be separated. Although the other pair (Feona and Kalinina) were also good, if my memory and passions do not deceive me, Kulchitskaya and Ruban had more fans. After the first performance I became one of them.

The following morning, I woke up with the feeling that something extraordinary, fabulous, wondrous, had happened. I was sitting still undressed on my bed in a rapturously dreamy state and recalling the performance, when mum's sister, Auntie Lida, arrived. She was a sick and lonely woman; she had once lived with us, but then everyone decided that it was better for her to live separately. She moved to a place close by, rented a small room in a private house from a very nice, but also lonely woman and often called on us. 'Auntie Lida,' I said, rushing up to her, 'What a performance we saw last night! And what actors!' In response I heard that the Taisia Kulchitskaya, who had so enchanted my mother and me, was renting from the same landlady as Auntie Lida. With great enthusiasm my aunt began to sing the praises of her new neighbour: she was beautiful, kind and easy to talk to. But the main point was that Auntie Lida promised to introduce me to her.

An opportunity soon arose. I was terribly nervous as I entered Taisia's room, but it all turned out to be very easy. The person who rose to greet me was a pleasant and unusually charming young woman of twenty-seven or twenty-eight; she was short of stature and rather full of figure, with large, dark eyes, an expressive mouth, wavy brown hair and an enchanting smile. She received me graciously, invited me to sit at the table, served tea, and showed interest in our daily lives. Of course, I have forgotten the actual conversation, but the sensation of kindness and warmth which Taisia radiated has remained. For all my bashfulness at that time, I soon felt at ease and left happy to have been invited to call on her more often.

This day marked the beginning of our friendship, which was warm and sincere, and continued for many years, despite the big difference in our ages and social status (she was a 'Meritorious Artist' and I was only a working girl). I often thought during those years, and later too: what was it that bound us, what made our friendship so radiant? It was certainly more than just the fact that I was a faithful fan of hers and devoted practically all my spare time to her. For she always had enough fans without me. She even complained sometimes that she was fed up with them and they gave her no peace. It is more likely that, having ended up in a strange city, with no friends and relations, she needed someone who was genuinely and selflessly attached to her, who treated her with warmth and kindness. That person turned out to be me. But there was probably some kinship of souls which made our friendship pure and joyful, with nothing overshadowing it. Taisia never drew attention to the difference in our status by glance or word, and not once did she ever upset me.

Taisia often took me to the theatre and into the wings, sat me down in a corner somewhere and said: 'Don't go anywhere.' And I didn't. But having finished her current number, she would run back, hug me, say something and dash off onto the stage again. There, in the wings, she introduced me to all her friends and partners. There, too, I made the acquaintance of Nikolai Ruban. Aroused and panting after their latest scene together one day, they ended up next to me in the wings. 'Kolya, this is *Zaichik*,' said Taisia on introducing me. She loved giving everybody nicknames. She called Auntie Lida *Tsaplya* ('stork') on account of her tall stature and long legs with inflexible knees and she dubbed me *Zaichik* ('hare') because in winter I went around in a hat made of hare's paw fur. I used to call her Taisia Valeryanovna *Kanareyechka* ('canary') because of her wonderful voice and habit of constantly singing.

It was extraordinarily interesting to observe the life of the theatre from inside the wings, although not always pleasant. I heard and saw all sorts of things. But I tried to brush off what I didn't like and enjoyed the music, dancing and the outstanding acting and voices of the performers. I often felt sorry for them. It was impossible to forget there was a war on and that, like everyone else, theatre folk were cold and hungry. The theatre was poorly heated; the audience often sat in their street clothes and boots, while the actors had to freeze in light dresses and costumes. I remember Taisia being troubled by boils as a result of a chronically poor diet and constant colds; her arms were all covered with septic and very painful boils. But she was not let off work; many of the theatrical employees were ill at the time. Before the curtain went up, she would squeeze out the pus in her dressing room, weeping from the pain, then cover the wounds with grease paint and powder, so the audience wouldn't notice, and run onto the stage to sing and dance again. And then during the interval the whole painful procedure would begin again. How many tears she shed on my shoulder in the wings!

Soon all my friends became true fans of Kulchitskaya and Ruban. One day five or six of us went to the theatre all together to see a show in which our common favourites were performing. We clapped so hard at their every entrance that by the end of the production our palms were swollen and crimson. But then it turned out, to our great chagrin, that Taisia had not noticed this storm of activity. Her performances with Ruban were always accompanied by loud, friendly, applause. Then one of the girls came up with an idea, which we put into practice on our next collective visit to the theatre: we devised some round metal discs, which we attached to our palms with twine. This time everyone heard us and the audience looked at us in bewilderment. We were extraordinarily pleased with ourselves, Alas, this time, Taisia just said: 'That was over the top.'

Taisia was adored by everyone in our family; she lived like everyone else. By the way, Nikolai Ruban was also a resident in our building, along with his family. Therefore, it was constantly 'under siege'; his fans hung round close by from morning to evening (in shifts, perhaps?), dreaming of catching a glimpse of their idol. Ruban was a wonderful family man, very fond of his wife and his daughter, who was still quite small, so the constant pressure of fans irritated him. And it was embarrassing for him when, for example, he needed to take out the rubbish in full view of the 'siege party' or pay some other essential visit. The problem was that all the conveniences (outhouses, rubbish bins, toilets) were in the yard. Earlier we had been hidden from general view by a fence, but during the war it was chopped up for firewood, so that everyone's doings were on display. You would go about your business with fans staring at you from all sides. Taisia said that Ruban was very distressed at first, but then ceased to pay attention to the maidens pursuing him.

While visiting us one day Taisia Valeryanovna looked through the window and saw Nikolai Ruban walking across the yard with his rubbish pail and asked me to invite him in. He dropped by and we sat drinking carrot tea without sugar. There was nothing else to offer our esteemed guests. I sat at the table with my idols, my eyes fixed upon them, full of admiration for both of them. Taisia was a very striking and beautiful woman. Her partner was a good match for her – tall, slim, good looking, with dimpled cheeks, spruce and elegant. City theatre-goers used to joke that Ruban wore a suit as if he were born in one.

Even my stern and unsociable father could not resist Kulchitskaya's charm. She asked me many times to persuade him to allow us to go horse-riding. My father had a horse at his disposal for work trips; in winter it was harnessed to a sleigh and the rest of the year it was hitched to a varnished two-person buggy. However, Father never allowed his family to use 'staff transport'. I knew this and did not dare to ask for it. But then Taisia insisted: 'Do ask your dad to allow us to go for a bit of a ride.' To my own requests my father would simply reply: 'The horse was not given to me for recreational purposes.' And that was that. Then I suggested to Taisia that she ask him herself. And father gave in!

I remember that fine winter day, with the sun shining brightly and the pure snow glistening like silver under its rays. In front of the house stood our 'coach'. We laid a large mat in the sledge, clad ourselves in huge sheepskin coats and, with the coachman in place, off we went! Taisia behaved like a mischievous child, continually prodding the driver in the back with her fist and shouting: 'Faster, mate, come on, faster, faster!' The horse was going flat out. At one point during a turning the sledge veered to one side, and I flew out straight into a snow drift! It was just as well that plenty of snow had piled up; it was soft and fluffy, so I didn't hurt myself. There I was, flailing around in the deep snow in my grossly oversized sheepskin, my sides bursting from laughter. And Taisia and the coachman were standing on the road and also laughing their hearts out. Then, together, they pulled me out of the snowdrift. We returned home happy and gay, dreaming of repeating this wonderful trip at least one more time. However, father was not able to let us or did not wish to compromise his principles again.

Also bound up with Taisia is my recollection of the day when I turned eighteen. In our family for some reason no one's birthday had ever been celebrated. But that year, as if sensing that within a month I would be leaving Uralsk and going far away for a long time, mum offered to put on a small celebration for my birthday. I invited several of my closest friends. Possibly, I would not have remembered that day if Taisia had not come. When I invited her, I was sure that she would not make it – what interest was there for her in celebrating with a bunch of girls! But she did come. Everybody was delighted, especially since the girls had not once seen the famous actress at such close range. Taisia conducted herself quite humbly and modestly. After a very meagre repast we were treated to a solo concert by our beloved singer. Standing me beside her and putting her arm around my shoulders, she began to sing; she sang a lot and fulfilled all our requests. The girls listened with bated breath, and I stood alongside, overcome with delight.

The theatre at that time was preparing for the première of *The Bells of Corneville*. In accordance with custom within the troupe, the performers did not have the right to sing any numbers from the forthcoming show anywhere before the première. How many times had I asked Taisia to sing just something from this operetta, but there was always the same reply: no, no and no. But this day she sang several arias straight off! Perhaps she too sensed something. I was not able to attend the première because I was already attending sniper school. But from a letter from my closest factory friend Yulia Largina, I learned that it was brilliant and a real triumph for the theatre.

A month after my birthday celebration we said goodbye; I was off to military service.

I can no longer remember when my relations with Taisia broke off, or how and why it happened. On returning home after the war, I learned that the theatre had left Uralsk, but nobody knew anything about it. They were not able to tell me anything about Taisia. But absorbed as I was in military service and subsequently providing for my own post-war life, I kind of drifted away from everything in my past, including the connection with Taisia. At times I began to miss her and felt the desire to locate her, but I had no idea how to do this, and everything stayed the way it was. As time went by the desire to see Taisia became more and more frequent. However, I didn't do anything to seek her out. It was of my own accord that, for many years, I deprived myself of contact with this wonderful and very kind human being.

Unfortunately, there are many things you begin to understand too late, when nothing can be changed or put right.

Fortunately, we did nevertheless meet, at a time when I had given up hope of this happening. One day, at the end of the 1970s, my sister Tanya and I went to Leningrad; she was travelling on business and I had decided to use up the remaining days of my leave and take a little break from my insanely busy work. We spent a lot of time walking around the museums and theatres. One day we decided to go to the Musical Comedy Theatre, having heard that it had a good troupe of performers. We arrived at the theatre, bought a programme, opened it and saw: 'T. V. Kulchitskaya, Meritorious Artist of the Karelian–Finnish Autonomous Republic'. I almost yelled out: Tanya, it's her, Taisia Valeryanovna!'

It was her all right – my dear, kind friend! How often I had remembered her, how much I had wanted to see her, and my dream had come true! I got so agitated that for a long time I was unable to work out what to do next. Finally, I found a scrap of paper, wrote a note with a hand quivering from agitation, and asked an usher to take it to Taisia. A reply came back that I was to wait for her by the staff entrance. It seems to have been a good show. However, I failed to take in what was happening on stage, as my thoughts leapt ahead at the prospect of meeting her, and I saw nothing but Taisia. She had an altogether small role, hardly got to sing or dance at all, but for me that didn't matter. I looked at the stage and saw the same Kulchitskaya – young, beautiful and enchanting.

After the show Tanya and I went to the staff entrance and stood and waited; I was exhausted from my impatience. And then she came out, immediately recognised me, and dashed over to me.

'My *Zaichik*!'

'What do you mean, *Zaichik*? I'm nearly fifty!'

'You're still my *Zaichik*.'

We spent a long time wandering around the city, recalling Uralsk and talking everything over. Taisia invited us to visit her and we gave her some exquisite roses, which even moved her to tears. Evidently the days when she was presented with flowers were already past.

On 26 February Tanya and I celebrated our birthdays and invited Taisia to the Moscow Hotel, where we had a separate room. We had brought with us everything needed for the occasion. We drank, had a bite to eat and then, at my request, our guest sang for us, performing my favourite operetta arias. Her voice was no longer strong, but it was still beautiful and she sang with such feeling, and her quiet voice sounded so wonderful that both Tanya and I experienced true pleasure. When we left, Taisia came to the station to see us off.

Tanya and I saw her one more time, on another visit to Leningrad. I remember a long night-time stroll. It was during the 'White Nights' and it was still light and very warm. We wandered around the city all night and split up only in the early hours of the morning, when our legs had given out. And we talked and talked, and remembered Uralsk, and it seemed as if there was no end to our reminiscences of those far-off times.

We began to correspond straight after our first post-war meeting and two or three times I sent her small packages. She was living on a very modest pension and her son, I understood, was not helping her.

Then one day I received a very sad letter from her. She wrote that big changes had occurred in her life and that of her son and grandson; she was disappointed that her grandson would not be able to proceed to the second grade. She wrote that I was the brightest star in her life and other such things in that vein. She was bidding me farewell. In the envelope were several photographs of her. The letter left me mystified, but it seemed to me that she was in a bad way, that something serious had happened in her life. I was very anxious, but did not know where or who to turn to. I received no further news from Taisia and only many years later did I discover that she, her son and his family had emigrated to America.

Thus ended my friendship with this very fine person, whom I sincerely loved and respected.

I often recall Taisia and look at her photographs. And each time I feel a melancholic ache in my heart – whether due to regret that all this is in the past, or a feeling of guilt that I could have done more for her, but didn't, or simply pity for a person who had lived such an impressive and interesting life but failed to achieve true happiness. Or maybe it was due to a mixture of all three.

Many years after the war fate reunited me with Nikolai Ruban in the most extraordinary way. One day, when I was employed as a school headmistress, the parents' committee organised a concert for the parents of our pupils to mark International Women's Day. They applied to several theatres with a request for one of their performers to take part in the concert. And Nikolai Ruban turned up from the Operetta Theatre! I did not attend the concert for some reason, but the president of the parents' committee, who had learned from me of Ruban's sojourn in Uralsk and my acquaintance with him, approached him after the concert and passed on regards from *Zaichik* of Uralsk! Naturally he had forgotten about *Zaichik* but he remembered Uralsk very fondly. It turned out that after his departure from Uralsk he had left the troupe and joined the Moscow Operetta Theatre. By that time my own interests had changed – in favour of the Bolshoi Theatre, the Moscow Art Theatre, the Conservatory; I did not go to the Operetta Theatre and therefore knew nothing about Ruban.

More than thirty years passed after my departure from Uralsk before I met Taisia again. But when we said good-bye on that day long ago in March 1944, we did not even consider whether we would see each other again. Taisia was unable to see me off as she was busy at the theatre. We made our farewells the previous evening.

CHAPTER 5

A Child of War

I was leaving my home town. Along with other girls from Uralsk who had been called up for military service, I was heading for the Central Women's Sniping School.

I admit I was in a sad state. Up until the last moment everything had been enveloped in a romantic haze of excitement. But when the time came to part with home, my parents, my native soil, with no knowledge as to whether I would ever come back here and see again everything that was dear to me, things became rather scary. Evidently this state of mind affected my comprehension of what was happening around us. At first, it seemed that we were surrounded by absolute emptiness and silence; there were only three of us on the platform – mum, dad and myself. And, somewhere nearby, the carriages of the train that would take us into the unknown. All three of us were silent – I because I was afraid of bursting into tears, and mum and dad, I suspect, for the same reason. My father smoked one cigarette after another. And it was only after the hooter sounded, and then the shouted warning 'All aboard!' that I suddenly saw the huge human crowd on the platform and heard the loud voices, sobs, words of farewell, and good wishes. We began to hug one another in a convulsive sort of way, kissing and chatting. And so, after the last embraces, the last kisses, the last words of farewell, we boarded the train.

However often I recall the farewell scene at the station, I always see the same picture: the dark platform, and the three of us – mum, dad and me. And nobody else beside us. But working on my reminiscences, it strikes me that that could not have been the case. My relatives, friends and those close to me must have been there to see me off. Not everyone returned from the place I was setting out for, not by a long chalk, and therefore everybody who possibly could turned up to see off those who had been called up. It was considered one's duty to those who were going off to fight. But however much I tax my memory, I always see the same picture. Amazing! I have managed to remember so much, both important and unimportant, but in this case – nothing, as if someone has blocked out this part of my memory and is forbidding access. Unfortunately, there is nobody now left to relate how it was in reality.

There were not many of us departing from Uralsk and we all fitted into a single carriage. The train moved off. The city in which I had been born, my friends and relations, all remained behind. Ahead lay military training, and then the front.

The Central Women's Sniping School for which we were heading was born out of stern necessity – the war. Its midwife was the Central Committee of the Young Communist League. It was at its initiative that a course was established in 1942 to train top-line shooters and in July 1943, by edict of the USSR People's Commissariat for Defence, the Central Women's Sniping School was established on the basis of the existing women's course. The school was subsequently awarded the Banner of the Young Communist League Central Committee and the best cadets were given presentation sniper rifles. In accordance with an edict of the USSR Supreme Soviet, the school was awarded the Order of the Red Banner in January 1944. This was how the school's contribution to sniper training was recognised.

The school was headed by an amazing woman – Captain Nora Pavlovna Chegodaieva, daughter of Pavel Chegodaiev, a revolutionary and lawyer who held several important political offices after the October Revolution. She had graduated in the 1920s from the Frunze Military Academy, which did not normally accept women: it took extraordinary persistence and obstinacy to become a student there. Nora possessed those qualities.

She fought in Spain during the Civil War, and had been awarded the Order of the Red Banner. At the commencement of the Great War for the Fatherland Nora Chegodaieva left for the front once again, fought on the Volkhov and Karelian fronts, and gained great experience in forming women's air-force regiments. Next came our school, where she stayed until recalled in 1943 to assist the diplomatic service in Havana once diplomatic relations were established between the USSR and Cuba.

The head of the political department was Major Yekaterina Nikiforovna Nikiforova, who had also been summoned back from the front. The graduates of our school always remembered her with great warmth and called her 'Auntie Katya'. I heard it said a number of times that when she showed up among the cadets, their spirits immediately rose and they gained new strength. The officers who became company and platoon commanders at the school came from different fronts or from hospitals where their wounds had been patched up. These appointments did not meet with the universal approval of military officers; however, in the army, orders are not contested but carried out.

Our school was a unique educational institute; we were told that it was the only women's military school in the world. It accepted female Young Communist League members between the ages of eighteen and twenty-two who had at least seven grades of education and a reference from their YCL branch. Among the cadets were not only those who had been called up, but Red Army volunteers. Prior to our arrival the school had graduated two cohorts and hundreds of women snipers were already fighting on various fronts.

TRAINING THE SNIPER

Though the Red Army had employed snipers during the Winter War with Finland (1939–40), the first attempt to train them in unusually large numbers is now generally believed to have occurred in the Leningrad district immediately after the German invasion in the summer of 1941. There was no shortage of recruits, as official organisations such as Osoaviakhim (Defence Assistance Union, with numerous shooting ranges and clubs) and Vsevobuch (Universal Military Training), theoretically at least, had prepared millions of men and women for the role.

Early in 1942, well aware of the desperate situation that faced the USSR, Stalin ordered that marksmanship and sniping, which had been left largely under the control of individual enthusiasts, should be organised more effectively. On 20 March 1942, therefore, the Principal School for the Training of Sniper Instructors was created. Its trainees – some volunteers, others conscripted – not only had to be at least twenty years old and physically fit, but also had to have completed at least 110 hours of Vsevobuch or comparable marksmanship courses. Renamed the Central Sniper Instructor School on 27 November 1942, the unit continued to prepare marksmen until the end of the Second World War.

On 7 December 1942, after much agitation from organisations such as Komsomol and many women who had gained marksmanship qualifications, the Central Sniper Instructor School created a separate three-month women's course. This proved to be successful enough to inspire the foundation on 21 May 1943 in Veshnyaki of what was initially known as the Principal School for the Training of Female Snipers. The upper age limit was raised to twenty-five, and the courses were extended from three to seven months. A great improvement on previous in-combat training, often ineffectual and the cause of many fatalities, this alone ensured that effective snipers were created. But only in the USSR was such a radical step taken: no other army employed women specifically in front-line combat.

On 5 June 1943, the female sniper school moved to Amerevo in the Chelkovskaya district. The first draft of snipers graduated on 22 June, when 104 were sent to the fronts and 125 were retained as instructors. A second draft began training on 25 July, shortly after what had become the Central Women's Sniping School moved to Silikatnaya near Podolsk.

On 24 January 1944, 585 of 887 second-draft trainees were sent into combat; the third draft (April–November 1944) released 559 more snipers; and the fourth draft, which began in November 1944, allowed 149 instructors and 262 pupils to re-enter service when the draft was aborted early in 1945 owing to the Red Army's ever-increasing ascendancy.

The Central Women's Sniper School closed on 10 May 1945. There had been 1,885 graduates, achieving 10,000–12,000 kills (claims vary), and more than a hundred of them had been awarded the third class Order of Glory. Losses had also been high, though are now difficult to quantify. Yulia Zhukova suggests that 250 of her colleagues had been killed, but it is not clear if this refers only to the 559 graduates of her draft or to the 1,885 women who had qualified as snipers: casualty rates would be considerably different.

The school was initially situated in the town of Veshnyaki near Moscow and then transferred to the village of Amerevo. By the time we joined, it was located at the Silikatnaya railway station, near the city of Podolsk, not far from Moscow. The cadets were accommodated in a grey, three-storey building which had before the war housed the social club of the local silicate factory. In its internal layout the building was more like a school than a club. The sniper school had extensive grounds, which were bounded by a high fence. There was a clock on the gate. All around it everything was remarkably clean and tidy, without a weed or a blade of grass in sight. Later we realised that this tidiness was the result of hard labour on the part of the cadets.

For several days we were kept in quarantine, and were then taken to some kind of farm, where we filled our mattresses and pillows with straw.

My first vivid recollections are bound up with visits to the bath house. One day some uniformed women with stripes on their epaulettes arrived at the quarantine building. They turned out to be squad commanders. We were taken to the parade ground, ordered to fall in, and escorted to a bath house in Podolsk. It was quite a spectacle! In my view we bore more resemblance to a band of gypsies than a military detachment. We were still unable to march in formation and keep correctly in line, so the rows got mixed up. And we were dressed any old how. We understood that our clothes would have to be abandoned, so at home, when preparing for the journey, we donned our worst and most dispensable clothing. The girls talked loudly among themselves, exchanging first impressions of proceedings. The commanders tried unsuccessfully to impose some elementary order, but nobody listened to them.

We passed soft-hearted women standing on the footpaths, who looked at us pityingly. Some wiped away their tears and voiced loud lamentations, others blessed us with a cross, and others still just stood in silence. The girls on the march tore off their hats, scarves and mittens and threw them into the crowd: no point in wasting good clothing; let others have the use of it. They accepted the items; life was hard during wartime.

A surprise awaited us at the bath house – a whole brigade of barbers. Deftly wielding their scissors and razors, they reduced our hair styles almost to 'short back and sides'. The girls had no wish to part with their coiffures, many tried to resist, and some even shed tears, but such tricks were of no benefit. Everyone ended up with the same hair style; we were all made to resemble boys, seemingly with the same look. The girls grieved, while the cleaner silently swept into a corner the black, brown and ginger tresses which had until recently adorned the girl's heads.

Following the bath, we were given uniforms. First to be issued was underwear: long, wide, white calico drawers stretching almost to the knee, with a cord around the waist instead of elastic; male calico undershirts with long sleeves and laces at the throat; and flannelette foot-wrappings. Then came cotton trousers and tunics, canvas belts, artificial leather boots with very wide bodies, and overcoats and caps with ear-flaps. Except for the overcoats and caps everything was ill-fitting, albeit new. Besides that, it was necessary not just to take the clothing and put it on, but also to choose it in accordance with one's size. As regards the underwear, everything was fine. But when it came to the uniforms, we were treated to a real spectacle. In the cramped bath house we would measure up one set of clothing against another, exchanging trousers or tunics; some found their overcoat too small, while others found it too large; some were unable to select the right-sized boots. Most of us put on the flared sailors' trousers back to front, which resulted in laughter of Homeric proportions. The biggest bother was with the foot-wrappings, which were impossible to wind in a more or less tolerable fashion. The girls jostled, yelled and played the fool.

Finally, everything settled down, we got dressed, and went outside to fall in. There is after all something about military garb that imposes a sense of obligation and discipline. We presented quite a different picture from a few hours earlier. Washed, shorn, and clad in uniform, we all felt different and carried ourselves differently. In formation we tried to keep the right alignment and march in step without talking; we even attempted to sing.

We were going home, back to the school, which really did become our home for eight long months.

Incidentally the distance between the school and Podolsk was not all that short – three kilometres – and if one considers the return trip, it worked out at a fair distance. In time we got used to it, traversing even greater distances, but at first the road seemed long and exhausting.

Along the way we had to negotiate a swing bridge over a river or a gully. The commanding officers would always warn us not to keep in step, or else the bridge would sway. For a time, we obeyed them and did as we were told. Then everything went haywire. As soon as we stepped onto the bridge, we deliberately began to mark time: one-two, one-two. The bridge swayed more and more and looked like overturning. The commanding officers got angry and abusive, but we enjoyed it. Sometimes we were frightened ourselves, but nobody showed it.

Such was the beginning of my military life. There were four companies in our battalion, and they were formed according to height: the tallest were in the first company and the shortest in the fourth. Following the lead of the school's deputy director, Major Nikiforova, they became known as the 'pencils'. I was put into the third company, and my friend Valya ended up in the fourth.

Returning from the bath house, we caught our first view of our living quarters, which were what was described in military language as barracks. They were a joyless prospect. In premises of no more than fifty or sixty square metres were two rows of double bunks flush with each other, two clothes stands for overcoats, two rifle racks, two small square tables, a couple of chests, and no chairs. Our platoon of over thirty was to be accommodated in this space.

The commander of the section was Sergeant Masha Duvanova. She had graduated from this school herself, so she had a good idea as to how difficult it was for us girls aged 18–20 to adapt to the new conditions, related to our problems with understanding, supported and helped us at difficult times, and cared for us. Masha never abused her rights as commanding officer, rarely resorted to punishments and, when that occurred, she felt just as bad about it as the actual culprit. During one of our post-war meetings she mentioned an occasion when she had assigned me extra duties for some offence. And when I was scrubbing the floors at night while everyone else slept, she had not slept either out of concern for me. I must admit I shed a few tears over that . . .

I have to say that washing the floors in the barracks was no simple matter. First, you had to take a sapper's spade and scrape off the mud left during the day by dozens of pairs of soldiers' boots, then scrub the unpainted floorboards with sand and water, and only then rinse them with clean water. If it was later discovered that the floor was not absolutely white and clean, you could expect further extra duties.

Neither Masha nor I remember what she was punishing me for then. As a rule, I was very organised and an excellent trainee, nor did I break the rules. Nevertheless, there was one incident when I was punished. On that occasion I received two doses of extra duties for addressing one girl in an improper manner. She deserved it. The thing is that sniper rifles are very sensitive to sundry bumps and shaking, and this girl had spotted a red berry on the firing range and crawled over me; her gas mask had fallen off and hit the telescope sight of my rifle. I was frightened. The instructor did not realise what had happened, did not bother to get to the bottom of it, and punished me. That meant another two nights in a row scrubbing the floor. However, I learned a lesson and for the rest of my life I only swore once, when, following encirclement at Landsberg, the other girls were sent to a different front and I was dispatched to hospital. I was scared to part from my friends and remain by myself. To my shame, my verbal creativity was witnessed by an officer whom I highly respected. He looked at me and simply said: 'That is unbecoming of you.' I never swore after that.

It did not take long to accommodate ourselves and work out living conditions in our new home. Everything was ready for occupation when we arrived at the barracks and we no longer had any personal property.

The bunks in our section had an upper layer. We lay side by side like toy soldiers in a box. But each of us had our own mattress, pillow and blanket. Our bedding was quite decent by wartime standards. True, the mattresses and pillows were filled with straw and the military blankets were coarse and a horrible grey colour, but the calico linen and napped towels were always clean and well washed. We were taken to the bath house every ten days and bed and personal linen were changed the same day.

For us this marked the beginning of a completely new life, of which we understood nothing at all. Literally everything had to be learnt anew.

One would think that making a bed was a simple matter. But when we began to do it, it didn't work out like that at first. We were supposed to arrange the blankets and sheets without a single wrinkle or crease; sometimes we even used a ramrod to check they were straight. The pillows had to be arranged in a row, so that not a single bulge stood out, and yet, as I have already mentioned, they were stuffed with straw. The towels were to be laid out near the pillows in a triangular shape; moreover, the bases of the triangles had to form a straight line. If the sergeant-major found shortcomings on checking the beds, everything so laboriously put together would be pitilessly torn apart and have to be started again from the beginning. Now I cannot even imagine how we contrived to create such an ideally smooth result with ten beds as we stood on the second layer of bunks, bent over almost in half.

It was even harder to learn how to get yourself dressed and shod, wind your foot-wrappings properly and sew on a fresh undercollar – and do it all literally in split seconds.

All these intricacies of military life did not come easily. The day would barely have dawned, I remember, before the command rang out: 'Reveille!' And everyone would leap down from the bunks at once, still not properly awake, don their uniforms in a convulsive fashion, and poke their feet into the two rows of boots standing by the bunks, each searching for her own pair. And standing beside the bunks would be the sergeant-major with a stop-watch in her hands, checking that we were within the required norm. Before we had even managed to dress in the set time, there would be another command: 'Retire!' We would undress again and go back to our bunks. Then once again the command: 'Reveille!' And everything was repeated from the beginning. We would barely be dressed before another command followed: 'Fall in outside for morning exercises!' We would dash out, still doing our buttons up or straightening out our clothing.

For a long time, the biggest problem was the foot-wrappings. If there was even a single wrinkle in them, your feet could chafe till they bled and the commanders impressed upon us that it was a crime in the army to have chafed feet. One smart Alec in our detachment found a 'ruse': if she did not have time to wind her foot-wrappings on, she shoved them down her boots (the shafts were wide enough) and stood in line. But then we were dispatched on a route march of several kilometres. She became a pitiful sight, barely able to put one foot in front of the other. She was subsequently punished for slackness. Incidentally, we had been warned about such things, but we did not believe it and personal experience was required to convince us.

Another example. We could never learn to eat quickly and were constantly hungry. We were well fed, in accordance with front-line rations. There were three meals a day, always including meat and butter. At every meal-time there was a loaf of bread to be shared among eight of us, and dinner always comprised three courses. But we were young, spent whole days out in the open, and the physical load was huge, so we were all constantly hungry.

The real horror was that you didn't have time to eat up before your platoon was called out onto the parade ground. We would leave the mess hungry, looking longingly at the remains of the food. We were repeatedly warned that no food was to be taken out of the mess, but we didn't believe it. We began to try it on; we would eat the food without bread in order to get through it more quickly and take the bread with us – wrap it in some paper or rag to stuff in our boots or trouser pockets. But the commanders were aware of these ruses; they had been employed before. So, one day, after we had come back from the mess (we always marched in formation), we were lined up in two rows on the parade ground in front of the school and the front row was given the command: 'Sit down and remove your boots!' Chunks of bread and sugar lumps spilled onto the ground along with handkerchiefs and other bits and pieces. It was quite a sight! Those of us in the second row began inconspicuously to transfer everything from our boots to our pockets. What naivety! The command rang out: 'Second row, empty out your pockets!'

That was another lesson for us to learn.

For a long time, we would, as the saying goes, step on one rake after another; our commanders would spend long, arduous days teaching us the seemingly simple facts of soldiering, and we would try to do things our way. In the end we would understand everything and learn it all.

In general, when I look back on that existence from the distance of the present day, I begin to think that there was a lot about our life as cadets that was absurd, harsh and simply stupid. For example, we were not issued with white undercollars for our tunics, and obtaining the necessary material for them from home was a big problem. However, it was expected that each cadet should have the essential number of undercollars and they should always be clean. Sometimes they needed changing two or three times a day; how were we supposed to get hold of so many? Time went by and we got used to it.

Another example. For cleaning their boots, the cadets were issued some sort of paste which was never going to produce a shine, especially on our artificial leather. However, the commanders did not take this into consideration and demanded that our boots must shine regardless. We came up with a solution: we formed a common fund from our monthly salaries of 7 rubles 50 kopecks and bought large tins of the best 'Luxe' shoe cream for the whole section. Our boots gleamed brightly enough to use as a mirror.

I do not remember that there was a special place for drying clothes, even though exercises proceeded in rain and snow. Sometimes we came back wet through and there was nowhere to dry our things. We used to lay out our wet clothes under the bottom sheet, carefully straightening them out so there would be no wrinkles or creases, drying them with the warmth of our own bodies. This method was not our invention, but we mastered the practice and employed it successfully. It was like sleeping in a damp compress. However, in the morning you would pull it all out from under you and it would be dry and as smooth as if it had been ironed. On this topic one of our predecessors composed a song, or rather adapted the words of a very popular school song.

> What a feeling, what a lark!
> What a night of rest!
> With my damp foot-wrappings
> Pressed against my chest.

We sang it with gusto, but what our commanding officers taught us was to get used to field conditions.

From our very day of arrival at the school we lived under a harsh regime. Reveille at 6 a.m. and every second day at 4.30, when we went to the shooting range. Physical exercises were outside in all weathers. Then came ablutions, bed-making, and a march in formation to the mess for breakfast – singing – and then back to the barracks again. There were exercises until dinner, and for that you had to find time to make yourself presentable – sew on a clean undercollar, clean your boots, wash the mud off your clothes. For all this you were allowed ten minutes. Quite frequently we failed to manage it all in the time available. Taking advantage of the fact that the orderlies in the mess hall were most attentive to the state of our necks and feet, we strove first and foremost to change our undercollars and clean our boots, while our hands often remained dirty. But one day a high-level commission came to the school. They called at the mess hall to see what and how we were being fed. One of the officers walking between the rows saw that one cadet had dirty hands. Immediately there followed the command: 'All hands on the table!' A real storm blew up. After that the orderlies began to check our hands as well. However, we were given no extra time to clean up; we simply had to hurry things along.

Dinner was followed by a long-awaited hour of rest and everyone enjoyed the pleasure of nodding off. Then came further exercises, supper, personal preparation, weapon cleaning, evening inspection and a final stroll (in formation and singing). Lights out at 10 p.m. And it was the same every day. There was almost no free time.

The first month flew by without anybody noticing. The school was getting ready for the 1 May celebrations and everyone was excited: on May Day we were due to swear the oath to the service and then take part in a parade involving the entire school. Every day we were drilled, taught how to march in formation and to complete the necessary moves with our rifles. Right before the celebrations we were issued parade uniforms, also made of cotton, but with a grey tinge rather than khaki, and skirts instead of trousers. What a joy that was! We modified the uniforms to size, sewed on white undercollars and strips of the same white material for under our cuffs. The white strips had to be sewn on the collars and cuffs so that they did not show more than the width of a matchstick. That was considered particularly stylish.

Generally speaking, despite the difficulties, the girls remained girls, enjoyed showing off and were eternally thinking up something new. Thus, they stuck plywood pads into the soft cloth epaulettes to stop them bending or jutting up. No matter that, when we had a rifle or gas-mask hanging on our shoulders, the epaulettes pressed incredibly hard against the bones and became painful. At least, they looked nice! We sewed ribbons tightly around the tops of our caps, so that the ear-flaps could not be released. Despite cases of frostbite, we still carried on cutting a dash in our ribbon-decked caps. In summer we were issued forage caps, but they were not new and had already been worn. The entire company became a sewing workshop as, sitting on our bunks, we replaced the linings. Then the caps looked as good as new.

On that festive day of 1 May 1944, we all looked simply magnificent, it seemed to me, clad in our new uniforms, keen and moderately excited at the prospect of the forthcoming celebrations. True, we had become unaccustomed to skirts and constantly tugged at them, but felt enormous pleasure nevertheless at wearing some semblance of female attire.

On command we lined up platoon by platoon on the parade ground in front of the school. To the sound of a brass band the school banner was borne out. The bearer of the banner and her two assistants – cadets from the instructors' company – marched with measured tread. They halted facing the line-up. In front of us stood a table decked with a red cloth, and on it lay a folder containing the text of the oath.

The ranks stand at attention. I am frozen to the spot with nerves. The oath-taking ceremony begins – solemn and moving. One after another the cadets go up to the table and articulate the words of the oath. 'Cadet Zhukova!' I hear. I approach the table with a precise step, pick up the text and, with a voice ringing with agitation, utter the words beginning: 'I, a citizen of the Union of Soviet Socialist Republics . . .' I sign under the wording of the oath, drop onto one knee and lightly brush the scarlet fabric of the banner with my lips. Then I return to the line. The next cadet is called out, but I am unable to see or hear anything, wrapped up as I am in my own emotions.

For me this solemn oath was of profound significance. I had after all volunteered for the army, guided by a single desire – to defend my country and my people. By taking the oath I had, as it were, confirmed my choice – to serve the people, and therefore it was very emotional.

Next came the parade. We marched six in a row, rifles in hand so that the point of my bayonet was near the earlobe of the cadet marching in front. I was extraordinarily tense; we had to keep in step, maintain our dressing and at the same time look to the right, where the stand was occupied not only by our own commanders, but also by visitors from Moscow, and to shout

'Hurrah!' in response to the festive greetings. I was particularly worried about one thing – stumbling and accidentally skewering the cadet in front with my bayonet.

Our parade was admired by the local residents, who came from all over the village. The ceremony concluded with a festive dinner.

Following the celebrations our exercises increased sharply in intensity.

Sniping is one of the hardest and most dangerous military professions. What is a sniper? What is demanded of her or him? 'A sniper is obliged . . . in all cases to hit the target without fail and with the first shot . . . To be able to observe the field of battle extensively and thoroughly, to persistently track down the target . . . To be able to operate at night, in bad weather, in broken terrain, amidst obstacles and landmines' (from the *Sniper's Notebook*).

Our tuition was also organised in accordance with these demands. Thus, the programme included training in tactics, firearms, parade drill, physical development and politics. We were supposed to know by heart the Red Army regulations and the ins and outs of all types of firearms – rifles, pistols, and both machine guns and submachine guns. We were taught how to set up fox-holes, including reserve holes and decoys; we had to know how to camouflage ourselves and sit in hideouts for lengthy periods, to familiarise ourselves with a new locality and to crawl on our elbows. There were special exercises to improve our powers of observation and memory, sharpen our vision and develop firmness of hand. We set about mastering the techniques of hand-to-hand combat and tossing hand-grenades.

Training took place in field conditions in all weathers – heat and cold, rain and snow, under burning sun and driving snowstorm. An exception was made for the theoretical studies – sessions on socio-political issues, regulations, and the operation of weapons. But then our political instructor, for example, also enjoyed teaching in the fresh air. Whenever the weather permitted, he would take us out into the yard, sit us down under an old spreading tree that grew in the school grounds, seat himself on a tree stump, and start the tuition. I remember that at first everyone listened attentively, but after several minutes you could see one head drooping, then another, and a third . . . The instructor would notice, get us all onto our feet again and make us flap our arms, run around a little, or otherwise stretch our legs. We would sit down again and within a few minutes everything would be repeated anew. Of course, this was due to our extraordinary weariness, but perhaps the session was not taught in the most interesting way.

Most attention was devoted to firearms training. Back in May we had already begun to visit the shooting range every second day. First, we dug deep trenches there, set up firing positions, and built elementary defensive works. What a lot of digging we did with our small sapper's spade! What a lot of earth we turned over! On the other hand, we learned how to do it quickly and well. We often moaned after all this digging, but the commanding officers would explain: 'At the front this is what your security, your lives, will depend on.'

I remember one fine summer day, when the sun was beating down mercilessly. However, we were still working in our thick tunics. The only concession was that we were allowed to take off our belts and unbutton our collars. Everyone was already exhausted from heat and hard work. A field kitchen arrived with our dinner – a big cauldron of porridge to be divided between four and a large hunk of bread each. With our spoons we took it in turn to scrape out the extraordinarily tasty porridge from the common pot and ate the bread with it. After dinner we were allowed to relax. I collapsed onto the cool, damp earth at the bottom of a trench that had just been dug and looked up at the sky. It was clear as clear, without a single cloud, and seemingly infinite. The girls lay down alongside. Someone fell asleep for a moment and began breathing heavily; others, like me, lay there with their eyes open and enjoyed the silence, peace and beauty of a summer day. I felt such calm in my soul that I wanted to cry. The hour of rest flew by in an instant, 'On your feet!' came the command, but there was no way I could snap out of my blissful state. Finally. I tore myself away from the ground, took up my spade and went off to dig.

Such wonderful moments were a rarity in a life that was burdened and strained to the maximum, and that is probably why that day has stayed in my memory . . .

The next step involved regular practice on the shooting range. Usually we would spend the whole day there, setting off straight after breakfast and only returning to the barracks in time for supper. And all that time we were digging, camouflaging ourselves, learning how move in swift dashes. And shooting, shooting and more shooting. We fired at targets from full, waist and chest height – at both moving and stationary targets, open and camouflaged. We fired standing, lying and kneeling, with and without support for the rifle; we fired both on the move and while standing still. All in all, you could not complain that the exercises lacked variety.

There was no restriction on cartridges for practice, but afterwards the cartridge cases had to be handed in – one case for every cartridge you had been issued, or else there would be trouble. This was understandable; cartridges were for real fighting. So, if anyone was short of cases, the whole detachment would come to the rescue. We would crawl along the ground on our hands and knees, looking in the mud and grass for the gleaming gold discharged cases.

THE WEAPONS

When Yulia Zhukova began her training in 1944, the Tokarev rifle, once the great hope of the Soviet arms industry, had been largely discredited; though never entirely withdrawn from front-line service, much of its importance had been lost. The 1940-pattern Snayperskaya Vintovka Tokareva, SVT-40, had been unsuccessful. Though its ability to fire rapidly could be advantageous when presented with multiple targets simultaneously, it was too complicated, too prone to jamming, structurally weak, and not as accurate as had been anticipated. Consequently, the 1891/30-type infantry rifle and its telescope-sighted derivative had been restored to primacy.

The Obr. 1891/30g was basically an old design, adopted in 1891 and then upgraded by the Soviet authorities on the basis of the short-barrelled Tsarist dragoon rifle. Usually known as the 'Mosin-Nagant' in the West, the Russians give credit only to Sergey Ivanovich Mosin (1849–1902); Nagant's continued participation arises from his attempts to pursue a patent-infringement suit against the Russian government when, in reality, little of his trial design survived in the Obr 1891g.

The Obr. 1891/30g rifle was simple almost to the point of crudity, but was highly reliable. Tests have shown that, in temperatures as low as -30°C, the action of the Mauser Kar. 98k, lubricated or not, will seize whereas the Mosin will almost always work immediately. In addition, the short-body PU telescope sight proved to be equally effective, the quality of the lenses being surprisingly good; conversely the adjuster drums of the German sights were apt to jam in extreme cold.

Several different cartridges could be obtained, though snipers generally confined themselves to those loaded with either the Type L (light) or Type D (heavy) bullets. The heavy bullet was regarded as more accurate, as it was less affected by crosswinds even though it dropped further as the range increased and appropriate changes had to be made to the sights. Tracers were rarely used, as they could reveal the firer's position to observers looking from the side. There was also an incendiary/ranging round, ZP, loaded with a bullet that ignited on impact, which could be used as a target designator even though supposedly restricted to air service. These bullets could cause dreadful wounds, and so were used only sparingly in case brutal reprisals ensued.

In addition to her rifle, Yulia Zhukova received instruction on a broad range of weapons. The old 1910-type Maxim machine gun remained the principal infantry-support weapon, sturdy, reliable, and surprisingly manoeuvrable on its wheeled Sokolov mount. Apart from minor simplifications intended to accelerate production, few changes were made to the Maxim during the war other than to add a large-diameter cap on top of the barrel jacket so that the coolant could be topped up with snow. The Maxim had supposedly been superseded by the PM43 or Goryunov, but the new air-cooled gun had barely reached service by the middle of 1944.

Girl with a Sniper Rifle mentions that Zhukova's sniper rifle ultimately gave way to a submachine gun, once Yulia had been transferred as the war drew to a close. When the Germans invaded in the summer of 1941, the Red Army was desperately short of light automatic weapons. Attempts were made to accelerate production of the PPD40, fitted with a drum magazine inspired by the Suomi type encountered during the Winter War with Finland, but the basic design was wasteful of machine-time and raw material at a time when Soviet industry, all too often in the throes of wholesale relocation, could afford to lose neither. The replacement was the PPSh41, known colloquially as *Papochka* ('Daddy'), which was designed with ease of production in mind. Made largely of pressings and stampings, the PPSh was robust and reliable provided that the drum magazine was not loaded to its limit: omitting three cartridges ensured that the magazine spring was not over-stressed and so minimised jamming.

The regulation issue handgun was then generally the TT (Tula-Tokarev) pistol, although some old 1895 revolvers was still being made when the war ended. The TT derived from the Colt-Browning, but chambered the same 7.62 mm cartridge as the submachine guns. This was effectively a Soviet 7.63 mm Mauser, used in the many C/96 autoloading pistols acquired in Tsarist days. The Russians, astutely, ensured that all their front-line weapons were of 7.62 mm calibre (0.3 in., *Drelineinaya*, 'three lines') to ensure that barrel-making machinery could be used for everything from the TT to the Maxim machine gun.

The TT was comparatively bulky, and therefore many snipers, men and women alike, carried handguns taken from the Germans. Compact 7.65 mm blowback types, in particular the Walther PP and PPK, were greatly favoured. The 6.35 mm TK (Tula Korovin), introduced in the 1920s and made in quantity for sports-shooting and covert use by the police, NKVD and similar organisations, was rarely seen other than in the hands of senior officers: judged from a combat standpoint, its cartridge was ineffectual.

Instruction was given not only on the Red Army's weaponry but also on that of the Wehrmacht, so that captured weapons could be pressed into Soviet service with minimal delay. The German Maschinenpistolen, MP. 38 and MP. 40, had been avidly sought in the early stages of the war before sufficient PPSh41 and then the PPS43 (introduced to service in quantity only in early 1944) reached the fronts.

A whole day of running, crawling and shooting took so much energy that you just wanted to drop and go to sleep. Your feet would ache, your eyes were sore from lengthy concentration and your shoulder hurt from the kick of the rifle butt. But you had to get up, load all your gear and head back to the school. Again, in formation, singing, and with full military kit: rolled-up overcoat, rifle, gas mask, sapper's spade, and sometimes something extra like a shooting stand or a target. Seven kilometres – in summer heat, with the sun baking down – but we were not allowed to unbutton our collars, or take a moment's rest in the shade, or drink the water from a village well. We were advised to suck a little salt. Strangely enough, it helped. And then suddenly we would be ordered to sing! What thought could there be of singing! Your thoughts were only on one thing – getting into the shade as quickly as possible. However, there was no arguing with the commanding officer. Someone would strike up a song and the others take it up; life would seem a bit more cheerful and the march not so arduous.

The teaching staff persisted with the same message: get used to it; it'll be harder at the front. When autumn came, and then winter, things got even tougher, and we often recalled the days of summer. But that was still ahead of us, and in the meantime, we were wilting from the heat.

As soon as we had learned to handle our weapons more of less tolerably, our ordinary rifles were replaced by snipers' models, with telescope sights. They were good rifles! We instantly appreciated the advantages of the new weapons, which would accompany us to the front. But they brought additional concerns. These rifles were more sensitive to bumps and more complicated to look after. And you can imagine how the sergeant-major checked on the state of each cadet's rifle and how well it had been cleaned after use. She would pick up the rifle, examine it from all angles, then take a piece of snow-white rag and run it along the whole rifle, from the edge of the butt to the muzzle. After that she would wind this same white rag around a cleaning rod and stick it into the barrel. And God forbid that after all these manipulations even a small blot should turn up on the rag! Extra duties would be the minimum penalty. But we looked after our rifles zealously, never begrudged the time spent on them, and therefore more often than not we got by without a box on the ears.

Route marches became more frequent. One night they got us up by sounding the alarm and took us in full military kit along the road around Moscow. We covered, according to Maria Duvanova, about 150 kilometres! In accordance with the situation that had developed on the front they were training us for fighting on the offensive. Therefore, lengthy tramps of many kilometres in full military kit, forced marches and cross-country runs were organised regularly. We were unbelievably tired but, if anybody began to squeal, we were invariably reminded: 'It'll be even harder at the front.'

I well remember my feelings after a lengthy march. The moment came when it seemed that everything had been sucked out of you, that you had no more strength for anything, and you were incapable of taking another step. Then suddenly the strains of a familiar march could be heard – you were met by the school brass band several kilometres from home. This band was attached to our school, but the performers were all men – professional military musicians. You heard the music – your weariness dropped away, you became more sprightly, cheered up, and made it happily back to the school. Evidently, it was then that I became fond of brass bands.

I cannot fail to mention one further aspect of cadet training at the Central Women's Sniping School – instilling a sense of patriotism. This was a major concern for the school command, the Party organisation and the Young Communist League. At teaching sessions, lectures and talks we were constantly reminded of our country's heroic past, of the fighting traditions of both the Russian and the Red Army; we were told about the feats of our soldiers, including graduates of the school, on the war fronts. Historical feature films were regularly shown at the social club. It nurtured within us a spirit of pride in our country and the desire, the will, for victory.

It is no secret that in 1943, when many old military traditions were resurrected, epaulettes were reintroduced in the Red Army. Many struggled to accept this innovation. Indeed, epaulettes were associated in our minds with the White Army, with those who fought against Soviet power. So that was hard to cope with! I saw epaulettes for the first time on the shoulders of cadets from the military school of aviation, which was evacuated to Uralsk from Voroshilovgrad at the beginning of the war. The bright blue epaulettes with gleaming wings on them looked attractive, but all the same I could not accept this novelty. True, it gradually became a customary sight and nobody paid any attention to epaulettes any more. But what was strange was that, when I was sitting on my bunk in the barracks and attaching the rough cloth khaki-coloured epaulettes to my tunic, I suddenly experienced a slight stir of emotion. I think this was the result of our commanding officers and political instructors working with us and explaining the reasons for and the point of this innovation. We soldiers of the Red Army had it constantly instilled in us that we were the heirs of the glorious traditions of the Russian Army and should take pride in this. Epaulettes on the shoulders were also a Russian Army tradition. And so we accepted the change. The sense of participation in our country's history and in the Russian Army, the feeling of patriotism, grew within us constantly and consistently. This in turn produced its own results.

This is what two-times Hero of the Soviet Union Army General Pavel Batov wrote about the graduates of the Central Women's Sniping School: 'Their love for their country made them staunch, endowed them with strength and energy, led them into battle. The Party and the Young Communist League had reared within their daughters confidence in victory, an unshakeable spirit, a proud awareness of their moral superiority over the enemy.'

It would have been possible not to mention this – after all patriotism would appear to be such a natural emotion for anyone. But the time has come when the concepts of honour, dignity and morality have been displaced in our country, and it has become almost shameful to be a patriot. Therefore, I would like to expend a few words in saying that we were brought up differently, that from childhood the most important value instilled in us was love for our country. Nor can I fail to remind you that both Soviet and pre-revolutionary Russia traditionally stood out for their high level of patriotism regardless of their social and material situation. Many representatives of the present-day Russian political elite are unaware of this feeling . . . If leaders like this had been in charge of our country in the years 1941–5, we would have lost the war.

I feel particularly sorry for the young people of today, who are constantly being deceived into thinking that the entire history of our country comprises nothing but errors, misunderstandings and crimes. In effect, our youth are being deprived of the right to take pride in their country. Many no longer see their future bound up with Russia and want to leave for another country. With us it was all different. In our minds the fate of the country and the personal welfare of every one of us were inextricably bound together. We all faced the prospect of defending our common future with weapons in our hands, and we were prepared for this, devoting ourselves to the science of war with determination and persistence.

Along with our training activities we had many other service obligations. We were often required to be on duty in the barracks or the kitchen and to tidy up the school grounds and the streets adjacent to them.

One day the entire platoon went out haymaking. I remember on that occasion that Katya Sheiko, the most domesticated of us, was entrusted with the job of cooking the porridge. When we met in 1975, we recalled how she had made her way through a dark forest at night to a collective farm field, gathered up a sack of potatoes and returned with this very heavy burden on her back. The forest at night time was scary and so was the prospect of being arrested for stealing potatoes. But she endured it all for the sake of making our food more nourishing and tastier.

Everyone enjoyed the kitchen duties. Basically, the work you had to do there was hard and dirty (peeling potatoes, cleaning out greasy cauldrons, washing floors). On the other hand, it was possible not just to eat your fill, but to provide your platoon with an extra ladle or two of soup and porridge and throw in an extra ration of bread.

For me the most difficult task was guarding the ammunition store. Sentries were posted round the clock: two hours on guard, then two hours on patrol and two hours' sleep. And then it started all over again and so on for twenty-four hours. It was horrible standing by the store, especially at night. It was located some distance from the school, on waste ground overgrown with bushes on all sides. Right next to it was a deep gully, also overgrown with trees and bushes. You stand there at night; the bushes rustle and it seems that someone is stealing up on you. It becomes unbearable, you turn around sharply with your rifle at the ready and shout: 'Halt! Who goes there?' You are convinced there is no one there, but it's scary all the same. You press your back against the wall and stand there, staring into the darkness, waiting. Then you tear yourself away from the wall, walk round the storehouse, and there are shivers going up your spine; again, it seems that someone is following you. After all, there was a war on and anything could happen, especially since the storehouse contained weapons and ammunition rather than study material.

In daytime, of course, it was easier, but at night, especially when there were no stars or moon, it was frightening. I got used to many things at the school, and there was much I learned not to be frightened of, but I could never rid myself of that sensation of fear when on guard. However, I never talked to anyone about my problem; I was too ashamed.

The platoon commander was Second Lieutenant Mazhnov. If we were lucky with our detachment commander, then with this second lieutenant we most certainly were not. He should be given his due: he did a lot of work with the platoon, provided us with basic instruction and made extra demands of us. This naturally showed up in practice. Wherever we were – whether at learning sessions or at work – we were always given extra credit. Within the company – and not only there – we became known as the 'Mazhnovites', but often with a certain element of distaste. This reflected the attitude of the cadets to our platoon commander. Formerly a collective farm labourer, Mazhnov enjoyed demonstrating his power over us and frequently humiliated us.

I remember the head of the school issuing an order forbidding the practice of forced marches (that is almost running). But our platoon leader contrived to break this rule. When we were off to the shooting range, for example, he would make us cover half the distance at a forced march, then halt and give us a chance to get our breath back, so we would arrive at the range in a normal state, having got our breath back. None of the superior officers probably even suspected what was happening, and a report against a commanding officer could only be submitted through the officer himself. Such were the rules. We did not dare to take this step, aware of our second lieutenant's vindictive character.

I remember another case. We had had a particularly hard day. On top of that, the weather was wet and cold. We set off to the mess hall for supper (in formation as always), but without singing. The platoon commander ordered us to sing, but we refused. Finally, he flew into a rage, but we were angry too and would not sing. For a long time, he marched us round the parade ground, demanding that we sing, but on this occasion, as they say, an unstoppable force had met an immovable object, and we stubbornly remained silent. Eventually it was time to turn in and we lay down in anticipation of some sleep. We had only just begun to drop off when suddenly the command came: 'Everybody up! Fall in outside!' Mazhnov took us out onto the parade ground and began to drive us round, again insisting that we sang. The platoon remained silent. We whispered to our song leader, Masha Zhabko, to start singing, though we had resolved that on this occasion we would not yield to the commander. It was impossible for Masha to keep silent because he could burden her with extra duties, but this would not have worked with the platoon as a whole. And so we marched around the parade ground, with the lieutenant ordering us to sing, the song leader striking up, and the rest of us remaining silent. On that occasion things did not work out for him. In the eyes of the whole company we were heroes.

One day I was the victim of a very unpleasant incident. We had been taken out to the field for tactical exercises. It was already autumn and cold; there had been heavy rain the night before and there were puddles everywhere. We were running through sticky mud which squelched underfoot and clung to our boots. Mazhnov was in charge of the platoon: 'Lie down and crawl forwards on your elbows!' I looked down; in front of me was a huge puddle. I swiftly took two or three steps to the right and lay down. 'Cadet Zhukova,' I heard, 'get up and return to your starting position!' I went back to the puddle and heard the following command: 'Lie down, and move forward on your elbows!' I lay down in the puddle and started crawling. To this day, when I recall this episode, I feel the physical sensation of the cold sticky mud creeping into my boots and into the sleeves of my overcoat. I was holding back tears at my sense of powerlessness, anger and humiliation. Then, scrutinising the cadets' performance, Mazhnov said: 'If soldier Zhukova had acted at the front the way she did today, it's possible she would no longer be alive.'

Later on, I accepted that the commanding officer was right in his own way, and many of us survived because we were taught the hard way, in conditions approximating to those at the front. But back then we did not like or respect our commander. He probably realised that and never attended our post-war graduates' reunions. Or maybe he was conscious of not having achieved anything in life and did not wish anyone to see that. We learned from one of our other officers that after the war Mazhnov had gone back to his village and remained a collective farm labourer. No doubt it was difficult for him to live that down.

The school command nevertheless found out somehow about the pranks our platoon commander was up to. He was relieved of his command and sent to the front. The second lieutenant came to say goodbye to the platoon, but none of us voiced any sympathy or pity for him, and it was a lifeless farewell. Possibly we were wrong; after all, the man was leaving for the front.

Our new commander was Second Lieutenant Irina Papikhina, a graduate of the Ryazan infantry college. She was also the one, incidentally, who accompanied our echelon to the front.

Women soon replaced men as commanders of all the other platoons. Things got a little easier. This does not mean that our loads were lightened or that we were granted any favours. No, simply that we were better understood.

Sergeant-Major Masha Logunova also left for the front. Everybody genuinely regretted that. The new sergeant-major has not stuck in my memory, whether because of her short stay in the post, or for some other reason.

We used to get unbelievably tired. But youth would have its way; the girls would play up, behave disobediently, take 'French leave'. Every transgression inevitably resulted in punishment, but that did not stop anyone. The girls used to joke: 'They can't send us any further than the front line.' The severest punishment was deprival of liberty: the culprit lost any opportunity to get away from barracks even for a short time, to enjoy a break from the exhausting exercises, to relax a little. But the most humiliating penalty was the 'glasshouse'. Whenever I saw some girl being escorted there, without her belt, I began to feel queasy. Fortunately, I did not experience either fate. However, even the other punishments, like having to wash the barrack floors when it was not your turn (which I suffered twice) did nothing for one's disposition.

Nevertheless, we still played up. One August day our detachment was marching out in full complement for field exercises. We passed a collective farm field with a bountiful crop of carrots. Suddenly from behind someone whispered the command: 'Squad, to ground. On your elbows, forward!' And everyone crawled through the field, hurriedly tearing the carrots out of the ground and stuffing their pockets with them. We then crunched through our juicy and incredibly tasty plunder. We ate them as they were, unwashed, as there was nowhere to wash them – just scraped them a little with our hands. And what about our sergeant? She was strict in this regard and did not allow anything like this to be repeated. But where was she? Had she gone off somewhere at that moment? Or, knowing that the cadets were always hungry, simply closed her eyes to it? I have no idea. When we met thirty years later, I asked Masha about it, but she did not appear to remember the incident.

Another anecdote from our lives.

It was summer and the heat was terrible . . . We were simply expiring in our tunics, buttoned up to the top and tightly bound with canvas belts. And, underneath, our solid underwear of yellow calico and long-sleeved under-shirts. We assembled at the shooting range, marched seven kilometres across an open field under a blazing sun, and the instructors gave us no relief; they were hardening us up, teaching us to stick it out, to overcome difficulties. Everyone was unhappy, everybody moaning under their breath. Suddenly, someone came up with what seemed to us to be a simply brilliant idea:' Let's take off our undershirts; it'll be easier without them.' But where were we to put them? Under our mattresses of course; there was nowhere else. We all removed them together and duly hid them, then went out for exercises feeling that things really would be a lot easier; our bodies would be able to breathe just a little bit. We came back and looked under the mattresses. The undershirts were gone! At this point we truly got the wind up. We realised that we had committed a serious breach of discipline and it would not remain unpunished. But the main question was: where were our shirts? And what to do now? Reporting it to the sergeant was a frightening prospect and owning up to the sergeant-major even more so; we were aware of her stern nature. While we were standing around nonplussed and discussing what to do, the door opened wide and our fearsome sergeant-major appeared. In her hands were our undershirts. 'Well,' her shrill voice resounded, 'who was the brainbox who thought this up?' We lined up at attention in front of her and waited in silence to see what would happen next. 'Do you think you have outwitted anyone, made some great discovery?' she asked sarcastically. 'It's been tried many times before; you're not being very original.' On that occasion the sergeant-major turned out to be in a good mood; she gave us back our shirts and delivered the sermon that was inevitable on such occasions. 'But,' she roared, 'if anyone tries that on again, you will have nobody to blame but yourselves.' At that moment I looked at Masha. She was pale, her lips firmly compressed but, in her eyes, I detected both wrath and bewilderment. Only then did I realise how we had let her down; for a squad commander was responsible for everything her charges got up to.

Despite all the burdens of army life and the exceptionally harsh regime, we managed to find time for relaxation and social activities. Our club constantly put on concerts, dances and film showings. Everyone chose what appealed to her. I, for example, enjoyed working on the company newspaper. It was my job to format it. The editorial group cooperated well and we succeeded in making the newspaper interesting and attractive. We contrived to squeeze twenty or twenty-five items onto a single sheet of paper. They were always laconic, precise and to the point. Incidentally, this experience stood me in good stead when I became editor-in-chief of the faculty newspaper at my institute.

Sometimes the newspaper published my own verse. I was too shy to read it in public, but I enjoyed doing so within a narrow circle, with the girls. I got a good response. Anya Vereshchagina, for instance, was sure that I would be a poet and, as she told me later, after the war she looked for my verse in newspapers and magazines. But that was not how it worked out.

Amateur performances were an object of general pride and affection at the school. Concerts by our home-grown artistes were attended not just by us, but even by the residents of the village. I particularly remember Tamara K., who sang gypsy songs and romances. Her performances invariably brought forth a storm of applause. It has to be said that Tamara made improper use of her popularity; at any opportunity she would try to get out of difficult and dirty work by citing her need to attend rehearsals, and she did take certain liberties. One day we came back from exercises and saw Tamara sitting on a top bunk playing the guitar and singing. She was wearing her tunic and belt, her forage cap was on her head, but her trousers ... The trousers, torn, as if a cow had been chewing them, were hanging down from the bunk. It turned out that Tamara had been on duty that day and had to wash the floors. Unable to find a floor cloth, she decided to use her own trousers instead. They were pretty much ripped to shreds. The sergeant-major had previously promised to issue her some new ones, but seemed in no hurry to do so. So, Tamara had decided to speed things up. We all laughed at Tamara's ruse. However, our sergeant-major, Masha Logunova, a fair-minded woman but very strict, had no time for mischief. She literally flew into a rage on seeing what had happened to the trousers and refused to replace them, threatening to force her to wear them till the end of the school course. Much to the company's amusement, Tamara had to go for a whole week in these torn trousers, which now resembled a floor cloth. The sergeant-major's wrath then gave way to mercy and she had another pair issued.

Generally speaking, there was no lack of wags in our platoon. In one detachment there was an Armenian – a good looking, slightly plump, and very slow-moving girl. One night, when the section was roused from its beds on battle alarm, she lined up in full military gear, but without her trousers – with her long white drawers visible under her tunic. The line-up exploded with laughter. We also woke up and literally rolled around our bunks in guffaws. Although she assured us that she had not done this on purpose, but was simply still half asleep, we did not really believe her and suspected that she was reaching for Tamara's 'laurels'. The company recalled this incident for a long time afterwards.

As I write about this Armenian girl, I am pondering over the grandiose conjecture that the USSR did not satisfactorily resolve the nationalities question, and that all our current national problems stem from this. This is all nonsense. Our sniper school included representatives of the most varied nationalities. In our platoon alone, for example, we had Russians, Ukrainians, an Armenian, a Tartar, and even a Greek. But we never considered who was what. We simply lived together, slept in the same bunks, made friends, learned the skills of fighting together and then fought together. And no misunderstandings, far less conflicts, arose on these grounds.

In my case, for example I do not know the nationality of many of my friends at the sniper school, nor am I interested in finding out; a person's value is not determined by her nationality. Our school produced two Heroes of the Soviet Union – Tatyana Baramzina, a Russian, and Alia Moldagulova, a Kazakh. Moldagulova lost her life when she took the place of her dead company commander, roused some soldiers who had gone to ground under powerful enemy fire, and led them into battle. Tanya Baramzina beat off the Nazis for a whole hour, defending a dug-out that had wounded soldiers in it. When her ammunition and hand-grenades ran out, they seized her, tortured her, gouged her eyes out, and then shot her at point-blank range with an anti-tank rifle.

We took the same pride in Alia and Tanya, honoured their memory in the same way, and it was a matter of complete indifference to us what their nationality was. It was only later that some began to work out how many Heroes of the Soviet Union were Tartars, Jews or members of other nationalities.

Time went by. We continued to train vigorously. The longer our training continued, the more intense the physical and psychological strains became. Some were not up to it. One girl deliberately maimed her own hand to avoid going to the front. Her guilt could not be proved, so she was simply demobilised and sent home. Another deserted from the school; she was quickly found, arrested and tried. The court martial took place at the school, with the cadets present. We were all indignant at the verdict – to send her to the front before her training was complete. We failed to understand why. We were due to go to the front in the near future and it was impressed on us that it was an honour to defend your country, while here they were dispatching her to the front as a punishment. We were spitting tacks, highly indignant, but the judges insisted on their verdict. Back then it seemed a great injustice, but now I am inclined to think it was just as well that the judges showed wisdom, ignored our views, and did not inflict a more serious punishment on that wretched girl.

I recall only these two exceptional cases. In general, the girls coped with the difficult training and, if conditions became unbearable, they would relieve their stress in less offensive ways: some would have a little cry in a corner or send a despairing letter home; others would play the fool, lash out, curse everybody around, or take 'French leave'. And even though every infringement was invariably punished, that did not stop anyone.

There was, however another option – to earn special leave as a reward for good work, learning and flawless discipline.

The girls used their leave in different ways. I longed so much for the comfort and warmth of home so I went to Moscow to see Auntie Nastassia – the former wife of my mother's younger brother. She loved me, always made me feel at home, and served up something tasty to eat (she worked at a petrol station and during the war this was considered a gold mine). In those years Nastassia was no longer young and had no family of her own, so she bestowed her kindness and tenderness on me.

We always prepared very thoroughly for a trip to the city; there was a whole ritual. After receiving the leave pass, we would proceed to 'clean our feathers': wash our hands, cut our nails, iron our parade costumes, sew on clean undercollars and polish our boots. The duty officer then scrutinised each of us from head to toe and made us march past him in formation and salute him. And God forbid that you should turn out to have a poorly washed neck or nails not well clipped, or an old handkerchief or boots that did not shine. He would mercilessly send you back to put yourself in order. Trying to dissuade him on such occasions was pointless – just a waste of time.

This forced us to prepare with maximum thoroughness for every departure beyond the school bounds, especially for trips to Moscow. I quite often heard from various people that the cadets from our school stood out from other girls in uniform in the most positive way. One day I heard just such a compliment with my own ears from the duty officer of a commandant's office in Moscow. I had been stopped by a patrol and taken to the office. First, I was marched round a paved courtyard for about thirty minutes and forced to roll my overcoat up (checking that I knew how?) and only then did they begin their investigation. It turned out that they had detained me for nothing, having unjustly taken issue with some trifle. Nobody offered an apology, of course, but as the duty officer released me, he asked: 'How do you manage to look so smart in an ordinary soldier's uniform?' He added that this was not the first time that he had come across cadets from our school and each time he had been startled by their excellent appearance and bearing.

I had a number of other adventures on my trips to Moscow.

One day I was returning from leave with another cadet on the same course. It was already late and we were afraid of not being back in time. We were in a hurry and glad to have caught the last train. And suddenly, at the station before Silikatnaya, we heard an announcement: 'This is the last stop; please evacuate the carriages.' What a nightmare! Nightfall, time running out, and still several kilometres away from the school. Convinced that there really would be no more trains, we leapt from the platform and dashed along the rail-track. By the time we got back to the school our leave pass had already run out and our delayed arrival threatened very serious and unpleasant consequences and punishment. Explaining everything to the sentries and the company monitor, we implored them not to give us away. The most difficult thing still lay ahead – avoiding the duty officer and getting back to our bunks without the sergeant noticing. My bunk was right next to Masha Duvanova's and therefore I had no expectation of slipping in unnoticed. I lay down quietly. Masha did not stir. Well, I've got away with it, I thought, but my mind was still troubled, wondering what would happen. In the morning I realised that Masha knew everything. But neither she nor the duty officers gave us away and everything went off smoothly.

There was one other incident. On that occasion I was on my way to Moscow alone. Sitting on the bench beside me on the train were two lovely women. They were questioning me about everything and oohing and aahing that such a young girl was going off to war. One of them took an apple from a basket on her knees, wiped it with her sleeve and offered it to me: 'Eat up, my girl.' So, we sat and chatted. Suddenly a young officer entered the carriage and, seeing that there were no free seats, demanded that I give him mine. I was obliged to do this, as a rank-and-file soldier had no right to sit in the presence of an officer. I was about to stand up, but my new neighbours intervened and then other women joined in. They abused him and embarrassed him and someone suddenly recalled the traditions of Russian officers – to yield their seats to a lady (me a lady, in military dress and leather boots!). It all ended with the officer giving it up as a bad job and going to a different carriage.

But one day, as I was returning from Moscow, I committed a blatant theft. It is shameful for me now to admit that I actually stole. At the school for some reason there were always problems with floor cloths. The floors would have to be washed and there were no cloths, and you had no idea where to get any. Neither the sergeant-major nor the detachment commanders concerned themselves with this problem and told the cadets to solve it them-selves. They did so as best they could, usually just by taking the cloths from one another. Then one day, when travelling back from Moscow, I got out at the Silikatnaya station and saw a large piece of sackcloth sticking out of a tub full of sand. Without pausing long to think, I grabbed the material and took it back to the school. For a while the floor-cloth problem in our section was solved. I have to admit I had no twinges of conscience.

The summer flew by in intense exercises and autumn arrived; it was rainy and muddy and it noticeably complicated our lives, which were hard enough without that. The twenty-seventh anniversary of the Great October Socialist Revolution was approaching. According to tradition a big festive evening was due to be held for the cadets and officers of our school in one of the clubs in Podolsk on 6 November. We all scrubbed up, ironed everything, put on our parade uniforms, and waited for the command to fall in.

But at this time, I happened to be hurrying to complete work on decorating the exterior of the school building. I was stencilling some slogan straight onto the wall in big red letters and drawing a five-pointed star on either side of it. When I started work on it I had no idea how difficult it would be. It was cold outside with a gusty wind and drizzling rain. I froze to the marrow, and my hands turned red from the cold and the caustic alkaline paint. As the work proceeded, I had to move the enormously heavy ladder further and further along, all on my own. I struggled to finish the work, got down from the ladder, took a look at myself and gasped. I was covered with splashes of red paint – on my overcoat, on my trousers, on my boots. I returned to my platoon looking like this, dreadfully upset at what had happened. I did not want to go anywhere, but it would be a shame to stay back on my own on a day like this. I headed off to the storehouse for my parade uniform, but it turned out to be shut, and the sergeant-major had gone off somewhere. I was nearly in tears from frustration that everyone would be going to the celebrations and I would remain on my own.

I had just got back to the barracks when the duty officer suddenly ran in and yelled: 'Zhukova, your mother's come to see you!' I stood transfixed at the unexpected news. The words ran through my head: 'My mother? Can't be. She lives a long way away. It must be Auntie Nastassia. How nice she's come to visit me! A real celebration gift!' I dashed off as I was, just in my tunic, with no belt or headgear, and without asking the sergeant's permission, and ran out the gates. It was categorically forbidden to leave the barracks without the squad commander's permission and, moreover, inappropriately dressed, but I forgot about all that. Running out onto the street, I saw Auntie Nastassia's fur coat some distance away, assured myself that I had not been mistaken, and charged towards her. And suddenly I saw that it was mum, my mother! I rushed to fling my arms around her neck and burst into sobs, just repeating one word over and over again: 'Mum ... mum ... mum.' Then I saw Valya beside her and her mother, Auntie Tanya. They were both sobbing too.

And yet I had had a presentiment of it. All the previous week I had suffered from some sort of incomprehensible pining and told the girls: 'I think someone's coming to see me.' It was an unusual state I was in. Whatever I did, this feeling of expectation remained with me. I would often go up to the window and look outside to see if anyone was coming. It got to the stage that, after dinner, when everyone else was lying down, I would sit on the window-sill and look outside. Since a nap was compulsory for everyone, the sergeant was cross with me at first, shooed me away from the window and threatened to punish me. But then, seeing how I was suffering, she let it go. I could sit there for a whole hour, looking broodingly out the window.

And now a miracle had occurred – my mother had come to see me. Back then it really was a miracle, because entry to Moscow required a special pass. But Auntie Tanya and Mum had arranged special work-related trips, each within their own authority, and made the journey.

As a rule, no outsiders were allowed in the barracks, but today they made an exception.

Auntie Tanya went to see Valya and my mother came to me. They had to see their girls. Each of us tried to reach out to our mother, to tell her things and hear something from her. Even if she was an outsider, she was still my mother . . .

We quickly had leave passes made out, so we could travel to Moscow. With Valya everything was straightforward; she was all cleaned and ironed, in her parade uniform, and ready for the journey. But I was all covered with paint and I couldn't go like that. Thanks be to the girls! The whole platoon contributed to my apparel. People gave different items – I didn't see what – but their common efforts did the job, and I stepped through the gates looking my best. Back then I took it as my due; everything seemed simple and clear: if your comrade needed help, you had to help her. Now I think: how hard it must have been to hand over your parade uniform to somebody else when you had the rare opportunity yourself of getting away from the substantial tedium of barrack life and immersing yourself in a festive atmosphere. Incidentally I don't remember how those who shared their parade uniforms with me got on.

But we were off to Moscow, happy as anything. All four of us squeezed into Auntie Nastassia's small room. Our mothers had brought us some civilian clothing and Valya and I were glad to shed our uniforms and put on dresses. Then came a festive meal. For some reason I particularly remember the baked tarts with jam. On 7 November we went out to see Moscow in its festive garb. I was clad in Auntie Nastassia's overcoat and one of her neighbours gave Valya hers. We strolled around the city's streets and squares, admired its sights and enjoyed not having to salute approaching officers at every step. True, my right hand kept straining at the leash out of habit, so my mother walked arm in arm with me.

Two days flew by in no time. In the afternoon of 8 November we went to be photographed together, and in the evening of the same day Valya and I returned to the school. The two mothers stayed in Moscow for a few days on work business.

I would meet my mother again – nine months later on 6 August 1945 – but Auntie Tanya was not to see her daughter again; in March 1945 Valya lost her life.

After the war Mum told me the pre-history of their visit. One day Auntie Tanya had come to her and said: 'Let's go to Moscow to see the girls. I have a feeling that Valya will not be coming home.' Mum got all excited about it: 'Let's go, we have to go!' With great difficulty they managed to arrange trips through their workplaces. In the end, they did it and they got to see us. It has to be said that, unlike Auntie Tanya (whose patronymic I don't remember, as right up to her death I simply called her Auntie Tanya, as she requested), my mother was certain that nothing would happen to me – she never even entertained the idea that I would not come back.

After the war Auntie Tanya no longer enjoyed meeting me and we rarely saw each other. It seemed to me that she regarded me as responsible in some way. Valya had a younger sister but, unfortunately for Auntie Tanya, she did not compensate for the loss of her elder daughter.

The November celebrations were immediately followed by the final and most exacting stage of our training – preparation for the exit exams. All our essential sniper skills were practised to perfection and polished up, for soon we would be off to the front. More and more frequently we were reminded of General Suvorov's words: 'If it's hard in training, it's easy in battle.' This was to stop us whimpering and feeling sorry for ourselves.

During this period, we were visited by girls from the front who had completed the course at our sniper school earlier. They shared their experience, talked about their successes and failures, gave practical advice, warned about possible errors, and willingly revealed their own little secrets, which any seasoned soldier always has in reserve. We gazed with admiration at those who had been to the front and admired their military decorations.

But at this critical moment, when the ultimate in strength, will and character was required, I fell ill; it was the most vicious case of boils. The most unpleasant thing about it was that huge lumps – ten or twelve of them – came up around my waist, under my belt. The pain was literally tearing me apart and at times it seemed that I wouldn't be able to endure it. But every morning I had to get up, put on my uniform, pull the belt tight and spend the whole day running, crawling, jumping and digging with the others – in short, doing everything that the others did. On the advice of the girls I tried a multitude of folk remedies, but they were no help. Then I went to the first aid station. The doctor got me to lie down on a couch, rubbed the painful area with iodine, took a pair of scissors and began to cut into my live flesh, opening up the boils. The pain was inhuman, just a nightmare. I thought I would not be able to hold out and start bawling. But I restrained myself. Then cotton wool dressings were shoved into the wounds and I was sent back to the unit without being given a single hour to come to myself.

Every day I went for fresh dressings, but not once after these agonising procedures was I able to lie down for a bit, to relax, to ease the frightful pains tormenting me, even for a short time. After rebandaging I would get up, get dressed, pull my belt tight (over a bleeding wound almost the size of a fist!) and go back to exercises. The 'hole' took a very long time to heal and had not even knitted up by the time I set off for the front. So, I left with this wound and a pad stuffed into it and en route went every day to the nurse to have it dressed.

There was one further horror to face: graduates setting out for the front were given very painful, combined inoculations, which were supposed to protect us against a multitude of illnesses: tetanus, cholera, dysentery, and other such 'charms'. For two or three days after these injections everything was sore: your back, your arms, your legs. We tossed and turned at night, trying to find a position that would ease the pain and allow us to sleep a little, while in the morning we all got up, doubled over in pain, with groans and lamentations. We struggled through the many hours of exercises with great effort. But even here we were granted no favours.

Examinations in all subjects began at the end of November 1944. We were not required to answer questions, but to demonstrate in practice our ability to operate in a battle situation: to shoot, crawl on our elbows, camouflage ourselves, dig in, administer first aid, function in a gas mask, strip and re-assemble a rifle and take independent decisions in battle conditions. It was in fact a very serious test of our readiness to engage in military action.

I cannot deny that we had been given a fundamental grounding in military operations, which omitted nothing that could come in handy for us at the front. To put it briefly, we had been turned into high-class professionals. Not only had we been taught military skills, but a lot of attention had been devoted to psychological preparation, developing our powers of endurance, and ensuring that we kept our heads, rather than presenting them as a target for German bullets.

One of our graduates, Lyuba Plyetnyova, happened to be present one day at the interrogation of a German officer. When the questioning was over, he turned to the captain who had been interrogating him:

'Can I ask you a question?'

'Yes, of course.'

'Which of your troops are they who shoot so accurately? Right at the head.'

'Those are our girl snipers,' and the captain pointed to Lyuba. The German did not believe it.

Our girls gave a good account of themselves in battle. They were responsible for the deaths of around 10,000 enemy troops.

Almost all the school's graduates were awarded orders and medals, and some became chevaliers of the Red Banner and the Red Star; 130 women were awarded the Order of Glory, third class, and fifteen of them received the second class award. And two of our number became Heroes of the Soviet Union. The commanders of the military units in which graduates of the sniper school served placed a high value on our girls – their military skill, courage, moral qualities and willpower.

Our remarkable school and its graduates have been the subject of books, stories and even a feature film entitled *Snipers*. I could not watch this film without growing tense; while I was sitting in the cinema, I must have sucked up a whole tube of mildly sedative Validol. Incidentally, this film includes shots of a girl sniper killing a Nazi. When I saw this scene, I gasped: it re-enacted my own duel with a German sniper! Was it just coincidence? Or had I told somebody about this episode and it had been used in the film? I have no idea.

And here is one more demonstration, albeit a slightly unusual one, confirming that we were superbly taught. Straight after the war the school was disbanded. The cadets of the last cohort, who had not made it to the front, were demobilised, while the middle-ranking and junior teaching staff were transferred to another military base, where they had to serve alongside men for a certain length of time. How those men joked and made fun of our squad leaders! But when it came to the shooting range, the women took first place, as they did in tactical exercises. Moreover, a review of parade drill showed that our instructors had the upper hand there as well. And when it came down to overall appearance, there was no contest. The time had come for our officers to poke fun at their male rivals.

Of course, war is war and many girls lost their lives. But if we had not had such basic training at the school, if we had not been subjected to such extreme, and at times simply brutal, demands, there could have been significantly more losses. Therefore, I consider it unfair that no credit has been given to those who taught us battle skills and should be held responsible to a notable degree for our success at the front.

We completed our training and passed our exams. I remember one test well to this day. It was the main exam and the most important one, and it required us to demonstrate the knowledge and practical skills we had gained during training and to show the commission that we really were professionals and snipers. Each cadet had her own task. My turn came up. Having received the command from the examiners (it was a large commission with representatives from Moscow), I duly went 'on the offensive against the enemy'. As I was running, I heard the command: 'Enemy machine-gun fire.' I quickly dropped to the ground, crawled away to the side so I would not be hit, and took the only possible decision in the circumstances – to wipe out the firing point. I gazed intently at the 'enemy' positions and looked for a machine gun. My heart was beating like mad from the rapid running, my hands were trembling from the tension and from quite natural nervousness. I looked and could not see where the machine gun was. Time was passing and I could not spot it! I scanned the 'enemy' positions from left to right and from right to left – I could not see the firing point. I began to panic. And then suddenly – there it was! I saw a small, carefully camouflaged gun-port and, in it, the barely detectable barrel of a machine gun. Now it was just a matter of technique. I fired successfully and hit the target with the first bullet, as a real sniper is supposed to.

I passed all the exams with the grade of 'excellent'. Like the other 'excellent' cadets, I was awarded the rank of junior sergeant, while the others became corporals. My epaulettes were now adorned with two bars.

After finishing the school course, I was offered the opportunity to stay behind in an instructors' company, training squad commanders. I turned it down, declaring that I did not volunteer for the army for that and I wanted to go to the front. Of course, they could have retained me there without my consent by a simple command, but they did not do this and seemed to take an understanding view of my wishes.

Shortly before I left for the front I went to Moscow to say goodbye to Auntie Nastassia. Quite by chance I met with Masha Duvanova and Irina Papikhina at the Kursk station. We had our photos taken as a memento and Irina later sent the photograph to me at the front.

During our last days at the school there were no exercises, although the regime was observed as strictly as before: reveille at 6 a.m., lights out at 10 p.m., marching in formation to and from the mess hall, invariably singing. But during these days we felt freer, allowed ourselves some liberties, sometimes even bordering on impertinence, and lived by the principle they can't send us further than the front line. I remember one day the sergeant ordered me to do something. And standing in front of the commanding officer, twiddling my belt in my hands, I cheekily replied: 'You do it first, Masha, and then I will.' Masha Duvanova even got flustered; for I had always been a disciplined and conscientious cadet. Then suddenly she literally roared at me: 'Junior sergeant, carry out the order!' I became embarrassed; Masha commanded great authority among us girls and we treated her with considerable respect. It was difficult to explain what came over me. Possibly, I was unable to withstand the huge loads of the last few days or succumbed to the general mood.

Next it was time to equip us for the front. And once again, now for the third time, we were issued with a new uniform. Apart from cotton battledress and overcoats we received wadded trousers and jackets, warm underwear and foot wrappings, and mittens with a separate pocket for your trigger finger that were suitable for shooting. We were also issued downy white American socks with elastic tops. They were very warm, soft and pleasant, but very impractical to wear, so that soon after our arrival at the front we threw them away.

We travelled to the front with the sniper's rifles to which we had become accustomed and almost wedded. Before leaving we once again tested their range, cleaned them, oiled them, put covers over the telescope components and wound rags around them so that these very sensitive instruments would not be damaged on the journey.

Graduation evening was a festive event. The huge school mess hall was colourfully decked out. There were lots of speeches, kind wishes, music and a good supper. For the first time there was wine on the tables. After supper we 'had it out' with the 'tell-tales' (there were a couple of them in our ranks), but not with any great severity; we felt sorry for them.

Finally, our last night at the school. Nobody could sleep. However, no one talked and everybody just lay there in silence. Our hearts were a little anxious. It was scary. How would everything turn out? What awaited us?

Our day of departure arrived, 25 November 1944. For the last time we fell in on the parade ground in front of the school. The school banner was carried out; the ranks halted at its appearance. There was a brief meeting, some farewell addresses, parting words and good wishes. Then the command: 'To the right! March!' The strains of a march sounded forth, the scarlet flame of the banner blazed in front of us, and the ranks firmly took the first step – a step closer to the front. At that moment I felt my heart suddenly beating as strongly as anything, and then came a hollow feeling down below. From fear? From nerves? From the unknown that awaited us ahead? Probably from all three together.

The column stretched for many tens of metres as it exited the school gates, following behind the school banner and the brass band.

Once again, we headed for Podolsk, but this time for its station, where our train awaited us. As always, when we marched through the city, there were crowds of people on the footpaths, mainly women, many weeping and some calling out to us. Everything as usual, except that we were no longer the disorderly gang that had strode through the city in March 1944, looking around in curiosity. We now formed a disciplined column, with full military kit, silent and concentrating. We were soldiers – all 559 of us.

Our squad commander Masha Duvanova was also bursting to get to the front, but they would not let her go. And on that day, 25 November, Masha marched alongside the column, next to me, and carried my kit-bag. This was not according to regulations, but nobody commented. One of the girls growled jealously: 'You would think Zhukova was the only one in the squad.' But I was the youngest in the squad and decided that Masha, who never allowed herself to single anyone out, had flouted her own rule on this occasion for precisely this reason.

We arrived at the station, where a service train was already waiting for us. Last goodbyes, parting words, and then, on command, we piled into the carriages. The train began to move.

It was goodbye, school!

CHAPTER 6

Into Battle

The war, the front ... Many books have been written about this – both fiction and non-fiction, some authentic, others not particularly so. In some of them the events of those years are truthfully depicted, while others contain nothing but falsification and outright lies.

The way thinks worked out, I ended up at the front only at the end of 1944. I was not there long, but I know what war is. With my regiment I had experience of being both on defence and on the offensive, of knowing in full measure the bitterness of retreat and the tragedy of being encircled for many days at a time. I endured bombing raids and both artillery and mortar fire. I froze in the snow in no-man's land, tracking down a target to hit, and got soaked in the Masurian Lakes area of north-east Poland. I cared for the wounded and spent time in hospital myself and subsequently, in the heat of bloody battles, I gave blood for the wounded. I made and lost friends. I escaped death by a miracle and was almost captured. Arduous experiences, physical stress and challenges to morale, cold, hunger, chronic lack of sleep, the filth of life in the trenches – all this is also part of war. And it was all compressed into several unbelievably taxing months.

And yet writing about the war itself is very difficult for many reasons. In the first place, so much has already been said about it that my recollections may seem trivial, commonplace and uninteresting. Apart from that, in the years that have passed since the war some things have been completely erased from my memory; many events have been, as it were, displaced in my consciousness and in time and space, and I cannot recall them in the order in which they occurred, or separate the important things from the secondary. It must also be borne in mind that I was a rank-and-file soldier and therefore the working out and implementation of military operations, even those of local significance, were beyond my ken. I saw the war mainly through the telescope lens of a sniper's rifle.

Ahead lay the front.

The train was carrying us westward. The 'us' represented a whole trainload of girls who were mostly scarcely more than twenty or twenty-two years old. Our train consisted of a long line of heated goods waggons, which had been used before the war to carry cargo and livestock. Now they were carrying soldiers. The waggons had bunks like the barracks, but no pillows or other sleeping gear. I don't remember precisely, but I think we slept on bare boards, spreading one half of our overcoats beneath us and covering ourselves with the other. In the middle of the carriage stood a cast-iron pot-belly stove. It provided a little warmth and we used it for cooking and making tea. For the whole journey we relied on concentrates, from which we boiled a sort of cross between a soup and a porridge. We had rusks in place of bread and salted herring instead of meat. When we looked wistfully into our mess tins containing the same pottage day after day, or chewed the black rusks, or sucked the herring bones, we invariably recalled the lavish catering at the school and sighed in sorrow.

I do not remember what we felt at the time, how various people behaved, whether the girls were tearful or distressed. But I do remember other things: the way we sang all our school songs one after another and sat for long periods by the open waggon door

– despite the cold – to watch the fields, woods and trees drift by. I remember what a pleasure it was to leap out of the waggons at every station to breathe the air, stretch our legs, and splash our faces with cold water from a well or pump. I shall never forget the simple Russian women who greeted us at the stations, woefully lamented the fate of girls from other families, and strove to treat us to their simple fare. We would refuse it, realising that we would be taking bread from the mouths of their own families, but the women insistently shoved things into our hands and said: 'Maybe someone will return the favour for my own boy.'

It was a long journey. At one point along the route a German bomber swooped down on us. The train stopped, everyone leapt out, scattered around a field and took cover behind some knoll or hillock. The plane dropped a few bombs and flew away without causing us any harm. The train went on its way.

Finally, we arrived in Minsk. Here we were to be divided into various groups. We were bound for different fronts and we said our goodbyes. It was very sad to part with Valya. It was not that we had any sense of foreboding, simply that we would have liked to have travelled to the front together, but we had done nothing to ensure this and we were repenting now that it was too late.

Along with my detachment I headed for the Third Byelorussian Front, which was commanded by General Ivan Chernyakhovsky, the army's youngest front commander. He was much loved within the forces and when he lost his life in March 1945 everyone was upset – both officers and soldiers.

Once again, we piled into goods waggons. First, we were taken to Kaunas and from there to Suvalki, which is on the border with East Prussia. This was the location of the 31st Reserve Regiment with which we were assigned to fight. We were met by a chubby, rosy cheeked major clad in a snow-white sheepskin with the collar up. He strode along the file and critically scrutinised us 'Well,' he asked, 'what have you come for – to fight or ...' His question was completed for him by the incorrigibly foul-mouthed Sasha Khaidukova: 'to amuse yourselves?'

Such was our reception. Everyone felt offended.

From the regimental headquarters, we continued on to join the 88th Division. At that time, we did not know yet that our 88th Division had a glorious history. It was formed in September–October of 1941 in Alma-Ata, which was at that time the capital of the Republic of Kazakhstan, then part of the Soviet Union. It was here that it was fitted out, provided with weapons, fighting equipment and uniforms. At first it was known as the 39th Rifle Brigade and comprised cadets from various military colleges and schools for junior officers as well as officers from the military faculty and students from the Kazakh State University. Almost 90 per cent of its members were Party or Young Communist League members. At the beginning of December its departure for the front was accelerated and it took part in the concluding stages of our forces' operations near Moscow. In April 1942 the 39th Rifle Brigade was re-formed as part of the 88th Rifle Division. The soldiers of this division eventually liberated hundreds of towns and villages in the Kalinin and Smolensk regions, Byelorussia and Lithuania, fought its way through East Prussia, and finished the war in Czechoslovakia. In token of the part it played in the liberation of Byelorussia the division was awarded the Order of the Red Banner, while for breaching the enemy defences and successfully invading East Prussia it was presented with the Order of Suvorov, 2nd Class, and the Order of Kutuzov, 2nd Class. The division received twelve messages of gratitude from the supreme commander-in-chief, Joseph Stalin. For its liberation of the city of Vityebsk the appellation 'Vityebskaya' was officially added to its name. Almost 20,000 of its soldiers and officers received orders and medals of the Soviet Union.

All this I learned only many years after the war in the course of meetings with veterans of the division, and also from the book *Vspomni, Tovarishch* ['Remember, Comrade'], which was published in Alma-Ata in 1987. But back then, in the winter of 1944, we were simply glad finally to have arrived at our destination. It soon turned out, however, that our joy was premature; our journey was still not over. We had no sooner relaxed than we were summoned again and sent on further. A very old, rattling truck was dispatched from the division to collect us; the back was uncovered and there were no seats. We piled in and sat down on the floor of the cargo bed. It was cold, the entire road was nothing but ruts and bumps, and the shaking was unbelievable. I had contrived to get a seat near the cab and therefore my back was continually being knocked against it. Despite the cold and discomfort my sole thought was about making sure I didn't bump my rifle against something amidst the crowding and shaking, and for the whole journey I held it almost horizontal with both hands. Agonisingly worn out by our ride on this wreck masquerading as a truck, we finally arrived at the divisional base and sighed with relief; we had nonetheless made it.

Our actual destination was the 611th Rifle Regiment. We were immediately informed that the regiment was one of special merit; it had been in action from the very beginning of the war and, as part of its division, fought its way through the whole of central Russia and Byelorussia. It had some major victories to its credit, and some defeats as well. The regiment had been awarded an order and had received messages of gratitude from the supreme commander-in-chief for its successful implementation of major military operations. Thus, we were joining a heroic regiment which had forged a distinguished military path and was very proud of this. Later, when we had already become 'part of them', our regimental mates were keen to tell us about the successful and not particularly successful operations in which the regiment had taken part. One day we heard about the feat of Sergeant Andrei Yelgin. It was written up in the *Pravda* and forty years after the war I read about the heroic act of this soldier in *Vspomni, Tovarishch*.

In October 1944 the regiment had been encircled. The situation was critical and a few days later the regimental commander received an order – not to hang on to the city, but to guard against losses and break through to our own forces. The commander called up Sergeant Yelgin.

'The banner must be removed from encirclement at all costs, Andrei. You'll be protected by four submachine gunners. They're reliable lads.'

'I'll get it through,' Yelgin assured him.

He then carefully removed the banner from its pole and just as carefully wrapped it around his body, put on his tunic and overcoat, and re-joined the submachine gunners.

Along their way the group came across an ambush and the soldiers were mown down by dozens of enemy machine guns. None of the four guards survived, but the badly wounded sergeant continued to crawl on, firing as he went and leaving a bloody trail behind him. His regimental comrades later counted nine enemy corpses resulting from that uneven contest. As they came to his aid Yelgin still managed to point to his chest and utter: 'The banner's . . . right here.' They tried to administer first aid, but nothing helped. Thus, at the cost of his own life Andrei Yelgin saved the honour of his regiment. He was posthumously awarded the title Hero of the Soviet Union and his friends in battle continued to fight under this banner in East Prussia and Czechoslovakia. After the war they handed it over for preservation to the Moscow Museum of the Armed Forces.

I remember it was an extraordinarily fine and sunny day, when we arrived at our destination. Our reception was friendly, but there was a certain measure of scepticism in it: they've sent us a load of girls . . . We were accommodated within a respectable distance of the front line in a small two-storey house. We had barely begun to organise ourselves in our new dwelling before an amplified voice suddenly resounded from the German side: 'Come over to us, Masha! Come on, Marusya!' It was so unexpected and the voice sounded so close that it was frightening. But the main thing was that we had only just got there and not even had time to unpack, and they were already aware of our arrival. How? Where from?

The enemy soon gave up this psychological assault and we relaxed. Dinner was served. Anticipating the pleasure of hot soup, which we had not seen for a long time, we swiftly sorted out our mess tins and started eating. At that minute a mortar attack began. From fear we abandoned everything, including our mess tins of soup and our rifles, and dashed down to the cellar. We finished the now cold soup later and cursed the Germans. It was embarrassing that we had left our weapons behind. This never happened again. The soldiers laughed and claimed that the Germans had specially arranged this salute in honour of our arrival at the front.

The regiment was in a defensive position at the time. There was no fighting; the Germans only shelled our positions occasionally and we responded in the same way. The scouts also exchanged rare 'visits'. Nevertheless, our defence was solid; the soldiers were constantly in a state of full battle readiness, and kept watch in the trenches around the clock.

During one of our first days we began to familiarise ourselves with the defence line – both our own and the German one. Several of us at a time went up to the front line and I was in the first group. We were issued white camouflage costumes – exceedingly wide trousers and loose-fitting jackets with hoods. Escorting us was a tiny officer with quite a gloomy look about him. The girls viewed him in disappointment; he was very young. We were young ourselves and we wanted an experienced, seasoned, front-line soldier as a guide. But when this young officer opened his overcoat in a seemingly casual way, we all saw a panoply of decorations and medals on his chest. This put us slightly at ease. While we were getting ready under the supervision of the platoon commander, the officer gazed at us sceptically, as if doubting that we were capable of anything.

Finally, preparations were complete and we went outside. I couldn't help screwing my eyes up: the sky had a winter clarity about it, the sun was literally blinding, and the snow that had fallen overnight was glittering like millions of starlets. It was like a fairy-tale kingdom; it was even hard to believe that such beauty could co-exist with a military front.

We headed for the front line. Ahead of us strode the officer who had been assigned to us and we followed, strung out in Indian file. The girls tried to give the appearance that nothing bothered them. In my case, to be honest, my heart was somewhere in my mouth, but I did my best to conceal my fear.

We had not even reached the front line before a hail of mortar fire began to descend on us from the German side. The sound of flying mortar bombs is simply horrible – a whistling, munching noise which sends shivers up your spine. Without pausing long to think, we flung ourselves into the snow. When the attack was over, we got up and shook ourselves. We looked round and saw our escort standing there with an imperturbable expression on his face. He did not say anything to us. We proceeded further, and again we heard mortars flying, and it seemed that every one of them was heading straight at me. Again, we dropped to the snow. This happened several times. And each time, as we got to our feet, we saw the officer standing with an imperturbable face. It seemed that, unlike us, he was simply not afraid and that was why he was acting so calmly and confidently. We felt embarrassed, but did not put any questions to our escort; what was the point when it was so obvious that he was just a brave man who would not 'bow' to enemy mortars. However, that turned out not to be the case. Having spent long enough watching us drop to the snow in terror, the officer finally explained that there was nothing to fear, as the mortars were flying to one side of us. And he showed us where they were falling. It was a long way away, a very long way away. Later we learned to distinguish by sound where shells and mortars were heading, but on that first occasion we 'bowed' to every flying, whistling object capable of bearing death with it.

Finally, we reached the front line. It was a long, deep, trench, almost the depth of a man's height, equipped everywhere with firing positions and observation points. From the trench, communication passages just as deep led off to the rear. Between our positions and those of the enemy lay no-man's land. But the Germans were almost next door – you could get a good view of them through the telescopic sights of your rifle. Sometimes a helmet would rise above the parapet on one side or the other. In the evenings one could hear the enemy singing and playing mouth organs. Those on the other side had a life of their own too.

It is difficult to describe what I felt when I arrived at our forward positions for the very first time. There was a certain thrill about it – excitement – but also insecurity, expectation of something unusual and, of course, fear. Back then during the early days I was afraid, in my own case, not so much of the Germans as of self-doubt; what if I don't know what to do, can't cope, make a blunder, become a laughing stock? Real fear of the enemy came later, when we were at close quarters with them and had begun to go out on assignments and take part in the fighting. But gradually I managed to overcome these doubts and fears. It would be more correct to say that we learned somehow to dismiss fear, to stop it dominating our feelings and will and depriving us of the ability to think clearly and act responsively.

I have often been asked the question: was it frightening during the war? It seems to me that this is not the right question to ask. Every normal person loves life and values it. As for the war, I am in agreement with the poet Yulia Drunina:

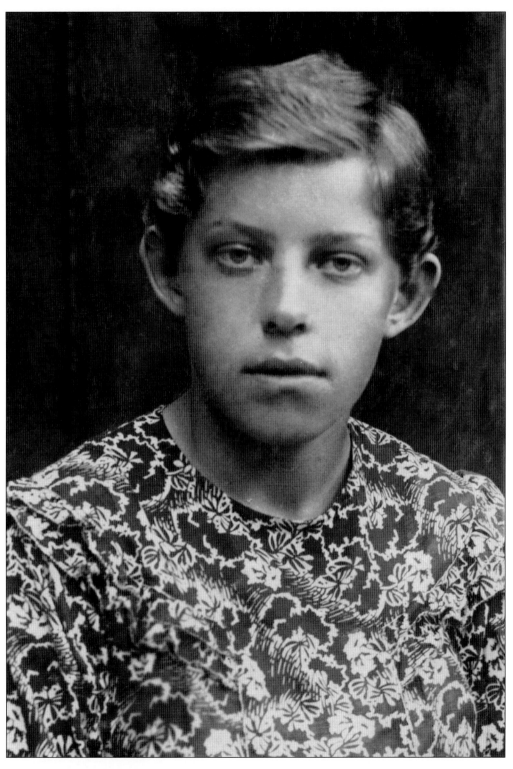

Myself aged sixteen, prior to starting work at the military factory, 11 July 1942.

My parents, Alexandra Ivanovna and Konstantin Sergeyevich Zhukov, in the 1930s.

Below & below left: My friend, Meritorious Artist of the Karelian–Finnish Autonomous Republic the talented singer Taisia Kulchitskaya.

The way we looked on arrival at Sniper School:
(*left to right*) sitting, myself and Roza Vozina;
standing, Anna Astrova and Valentina Shipova,
10 April 1944.

Our platoon. In the centre, Platoon Commander Second Lieutenant Mazhnov, May 1944.
I am immediately to the right of Mazhnov, in the second row.

Above: Our squad. In the centre, Sergeant Masha Duvanova,
August 1944.

Left: We have just received our sniper's rifles.
On my right is Lyuba Ruzhitskaya,
June 1944.

With Platoon Commander Second Lieutenant Irina Papikhina (*seated right*) and Squad Commander Sergeant Masha Duvanova (*seated left*) prior to departure for the front, November 1944.

A farewell photo with Company Sergeant-Major Masha Logunova (*2nd left, 2nd row*), who left for the front before we did.

A studio portrait with my mother when she visited me at the Sniper School before my departure for the front, November 1944.

Masha Duvanova and me outside the former Sniper School building near Silikatnaya station in the late 1970s.

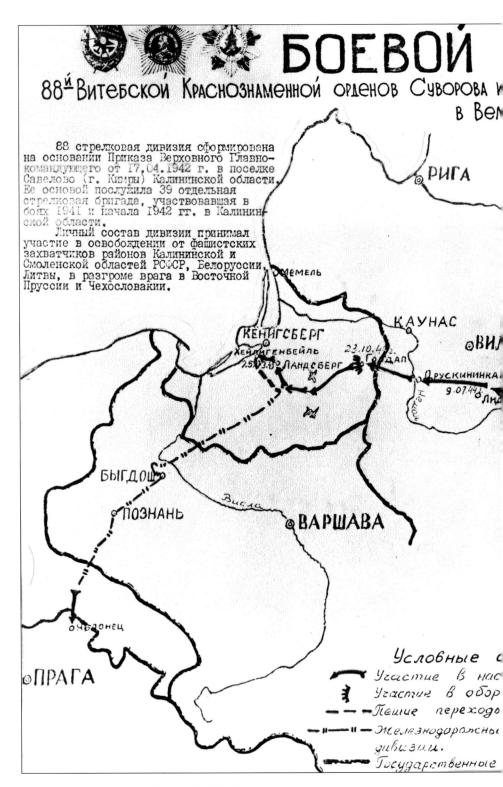

Map of the 88th Rifle Division's progress westward.

ПУТЬ

узова II степени стрелковой дивизии
й Отечественной войне

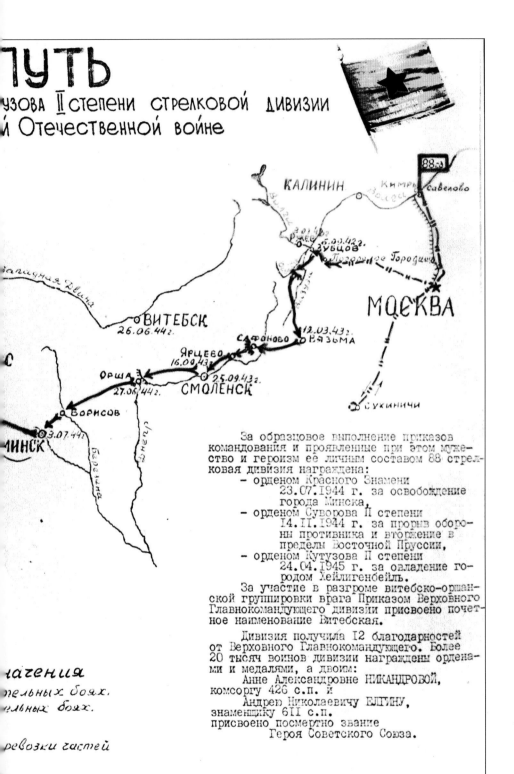

За образцовое выполнение приказов командования и проявленные при этом мужество и героизм ее личным составом 88 стрелковая дивизия награждена:

- орденом Красного Знамени 23.07.1944 г. за освобождение города Минска,
- орденом Суворова II степени 14.11.1944 г. за прорыв обороны противника и вторжение в пределы Восточной Пруссии,
- орденом Кутузова II степени 24.04.1945 г. за овладение городом Хейлигенбейль.

За участие в разгроме витебско-оршанской группировки врага Приказом Верховного Главнокомандующего дивизии присвоено почетное наименование Витебская.

Дивизия получила 12 благодарностей от Верховного Главнокомандующего. Более 20 тысяч воинов дивизии награждены орденами и медалями, а двоим:

Анне Александровне НИКАНДРОВОЙ, комсоргу 426 с.п. и

Андрею Николаевичу ЕЛГИНУ, знаменщику 611 с.п. присвоено посмертно звание Героя Советского Союза.

ачения

пельных боях.
льных боях.

ревозки частей

лицы

With my regimental 'knights in shining armour': seated, from left Vasily Stolbov, myself, Pyotr Chirkov, and lying in front Alexei Popov. Geidau, East Prussia, 20 June 1945.

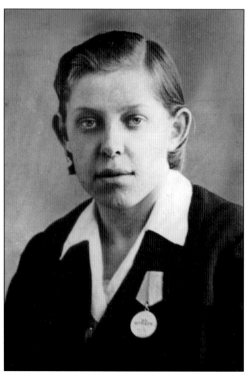

A photo of me after I was presented with my medal 'For Bravery'. I was not able to receive this at the front so I was given it at the Uralsk military commissariat after my return home in 1945.

With Masha Duvanova. Our first meeting in thirty years, 1975.

A group of Sniper School graduates in Red Square during our 1975 reunion.

My old squad, almost at full strength, seen at our first reunion in 1975.

Above, My Red Army booklet and, *below*, my Sniper School graduation certificate.

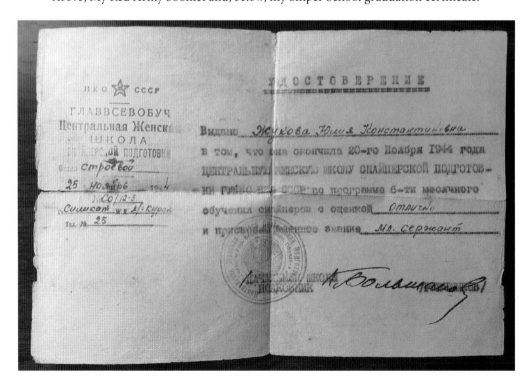

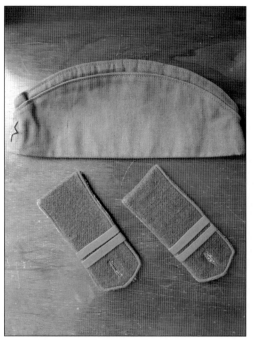

My Army cap and epaulettes.

Above & below: My awards of the war and post-war periods.

Enjoying the company of my family: *left to right*, my great-granddaughter
Margarita, granddaughter Varvara, myself, and my daughter Olga
with the family favourite, Janny the Spitz,
Victory Day, 9 May 2018.

Anyone who claims that war's not scary,
Knows not the actuality of war.

On that memorable winter day in 1944 we went out onto the front line for the first time. We were shown the enemy firing positions, got to know the German pattern of life, which they unwaveringly stuck to. The most dangerous sectors were pointed out – mostly those which were most frequently fired upon by the Germans – and we were informed that a sniper had quite recently appeared on the other side.

We were soon convinced of that ourselves: a few days after our arrival one of our girls was fatally struck by a precise bullet to the head. We took this first death very badly. It was all aggravated even further by the fact that, on the way to the front, this girl had got involved in some unpleasant conflict with our officers and someone had voiced an unfavourable wish in her direction. Now we all felt guilty about her and it was a long time before we were able to rid ourselves of this feeling. And the girl who had actually said the unkind words kept insisting: 'It's all my fault. I'm to blame.'

Such was the beginning of our life at the front. But, despite our anxiety, we could not allow ourselves to relax; we had a job to do. Every day we went out to the front line, learned how to see and hear, to recognise enemy firing points. We selected firing positions from which we could best hit enemy targets and worked out the approximate distances to them. We quickly made friends with the scouts, who willingly helped us to familiarise ourselves with the environment. We had a lot in common; we were both engaged in an occupation that was kind of like 'piece work' and both we and the scouts constantly found ourselves face to face with danger (they on surveillance, and we while stalking). Even in defence, when the environment was more or less calm, we were at risk every day. We also had common 'privileges': both they and we were served hot food and vodka at the head of the queue because we were constantly on the job, sometimes spending whole days lying in the cold, in the snow. True, the girls generally turned down the allotted hundred grams and handed the vodka over to our friends, the scouts. They would return the favour, often treating us to sweets and other tasty morsels they had captured. The chief thing was that they willingly shared their experience with us and taught us the wisdom of the front. As scouts, they knew the German defences better than we did and they passed all this information on to us.

Generally speaking, we were true friends to one another and always got worried and agitated when one of the girls or the scouts was away on an assignment. We marked the start of the new year, 1945, together. But all I can remember from that evening is the sight of two of our girls standing under a torn umbrella obtained from heaven knows where, singing a stupid comic song.

> Three hours we've been standing here, soaking in
> the rain.
> Three hours in the same old place, just waiting, what
> a pain!
> Peace and quiet day or night we'll never see again.
> Just two of us, and clearly,
> We love each other dearly . . .

And so on. However, I also recall the tin mugs of vodka on a home-made table, and a gramophone in the corner. We danced to its tinkling sounds. And I recall that on account of the special occasion we took off the wadded trousers we were sick to death of. What we put on instead – other trousers or skirts – I don't remember.

My baptism of fire had taken place before New Year; I killed my first German.

My partner and I were out on a mission as usual. Because we had no experience, we were not permitted to go beyond the defence line; we were supposed to stay in a trench, study the enemy defences, spot their firing and observation points, observe any possible German movements, and determine potential targets for a subsequent strike. We were allowed to shoot only in exceptional circumstances and only if we were certain of the target.

That day our watch on the forward line was extended, we were already freezing and tired, but we did not go back. Suddenly, I saw – directly opposite us, in a trench leading from the rear to the forward line – a German walking at full height, without even stooping. This sector of the enemy forward line was open, everything was plainly visible, and therefore the Germans always hurried along it as quickly as possible and ducked extra low. But this man – whether he had only just arrived or was just foolhardy – was walking at full height and unhurriedly. I took the decision to fire! Holding my breath, I took careful aim and smoothly pressed the trigger. The German waved his arms in an absurd manner and somehow collapsed to the side. My partner and I waited a little and then withdrew, after asking the soldiers to keep an eye on the German. The next day they said that they had observed the German for a long time, to see if he would get up again, but he had not done so and by dusk nobody had come for him. In fact, no movements out of the ordinary were observed. Evidently, I had hit the target. We reported it to the command. In the evening the whole detachment was lined up and I was publicly thanked.

I was overcome by a complex of emotions that day. On the one, hand I was glad to have opened my wartime tally. On the other hand, when you kill a human being, even an enemy, you feel uneasy. I remember that evening feeling slightly nauseous and shivery; I did not want to think about the dead man.

Then it all passed. I got to see so many evil things committed by the Nazis that I felt no pity for those I killed. It is frightening to admit it, but wiping out an enemy became just a job, a duty which had to be well performed. Otherwise they would kill you.

No sooner had I finished writing this story than something very strange happened. I was busily selecting photographs to make a special album to illustrate the period of my life I was describing, back in March 2000, when I came across a letter which I had sent off from the front exactly fifty-five years earlier – on 1 March 1945 – to my old friend from the factory, Yulia Largina.

Many years later, though I don't remember in what connection, she had sent this letter back to me in Moscow. I found myself holding a typical letter from the front. I opened it and slowly read it through. To my surprise, I learned that my first Nazi victim had not been killed in the way I described above. It turned out that the sequence of events was quite different:

> You ask what I felt before my first battle. It is difficult even to put it into words. I was nervous, but sometimes I was affected by feelings of indifference. I felt that whatever would be would be. I now have to my credit not just two Fritzes, but more. I have wiped out four Fritzes while on defence and I don't know how many while on the offensive; I didn't count them. All in all, my tally is rising. It is difficult to describe that first battle, but I can tell you how I killed my first Fritz.
>
> It happened while I was on defence. It was a superb day. The sun was shining brightly and the snow was sparkling in the fields. We had just had new camouflage suits issued, put them on, and gone out stalking. On we went, all of the same height, all in the same costumes, like bear cubs. We cautiously approached our trenches, jumped in and took up our posts. It was the first time we had been out stalking. I was very nervous; up until now I had not even seen a Fritz. And there we stood – one hour, two, three, four – and I still didn't see anyone. I was beginning to

worry that we wouldn't even see anyone, never mind kill them. It was about three o'clock in the afternoon when my observer called out: 'Fritzes!' My vision went black. I pressed my eye to the lenses and saw two Fritzes coming out of a wood – walking at full height. And I had a good clear view of them. I felt myself struggling for breath. I fired, but I had hurried and missed. I quickly reloaded the rifle and fired again. This time the bullet hit the mark. One Fritz fell, while the other managed to sneak off into the wood. And although I saw it with my own eyes and others saw it, I could not believe that I had killed a Fritz with my own hands. What a mood I was in as I walked back! The girls came to congratulate me. The company commander voiced his gratitude. The first digit appeared on my sniper's card. That was how I opened my tally.

So that is how it was the first time. Clearly, my original recollections were flawed and, had that letter not survived by a miracle, I would probably never have been any the wiser. But to me the episode I described earlier really did happen. I remember it distinctly and feel it with my own skin, if I can put it like that; I can physically sense what I was going through on that occasion. Possibly, my heightened perception of that incident was due to some special circumstances. Therefore, I have decided not to change anything in the text. Let the original version remain the way I remember it.

My total score comprises eight dead Nazis. But how is one supposed to count them in fact? When we were encircled at Landsberg, we did not leave our trenches for days, repelled six or eight German attacks a day, and fired and fired until our eyes grew dark. How could it be determined how many had been killed and by whom? I kept firing, the soldiers in the trench beside me kept firing, the machine guns were firing . . . How can you calculate how many fell from your bullets? Therefore,

I have always approached such tallies with a certain measure of scepticism. This does not mean that I have doubts about the achievements of those who wiped out dozens of Nazis with a sniper's rifle. I simply counted things my own way. Therefore, my eight victims represent what was confirmed by observers and, basically, they were targets destroyed on orders.

Such was the case on that occasion when I was ordered to wipe out an enemy sniper who had arrived in our regiment's sector a short time earlier and was causing us a great deal of unpleasantness.

One day my partner and I were called up by the commander. An order had come through: to wipe out that German sniper at all costs. The choice fell on us.

Having been given the order, we set about carefully preparing for this dangerous and responsible operation. We all realised that our enemy was a very experienced sniper, way above our class. He proved impossible to spot; he would fire and disappear as if he had melted away, and sometimes he would not appear for several days. He would re-appear after a while, but in a different location. And every time he fired from a new position. It was going to be a difficult contest. Therefore, with the help of our scout friends we thoroughly staked out the German defensive line in our sector, visually feeling it out metre by metre, and worked out where the sniper could appear from. We chose several firing positions for ourselves. We did not have a lot of experience and therefore our preparations had to be very thorough.

Then came the deciding day, when we went out to the front line with a clear goal – to stalk a German sniper. We took up our positions; I was in a machine-gun nest, and in a trench a little further away from me was my partner. We stood there, waiting and observing. Time passed slowly. It was getting cold, but running on the spot or even moving was out of the question; you could miss the enemy or give yourself away. Our 'neighbours' were silent – no movement, no shooting. Given the frost we had had, they were probably freezing too. We were already tired and chilled to the bone, and our eyes had begun to water from the tension. Suddenly I had an idea. 'Lift your cap up over the parapet,' I told my partner. Quickly cottoning on what to do, she walked three or four metres away from me, put some sort of cap on a stick, raised it slightly over the parapet, lowered it and raised it again a few steps away, as if to represent somebody walking along the trench. The distinct, dry crackling sound of a shot rang out – a direct hit on the cap. Just a single shot; it was not followed up. It was him! From the sound I was able to determine roughly where the shot came from. I looked in that direction. In no-man's land, at a slight angle from me, a bush seemed to sway a little. But no, it wasn't even a bush; rather, a shadow on the snow which flashed by and froze. So, that was where he was! I took aim and fired. Immediately I changed my position and pressed against the window in the gun-port. Now I could clearly see the bush sway and snow drop from it. Then it swayed once more and that was it. My partner and I continued our observation, and the soldiers in the trench also waited with interest to see what would happen. Nothing. All was quiet and peaceful. Nobody on the other side responded to my shot, even though our shots usually drew a volley in response.

Dusk was already falling when we returned from the front line. Tired and frozen, we were still a little excited; we wanted to know the results of our operation.

But in the early morning of the following day the Germans unleashed a frantic hail of fire on that sector in which my partner and I had begun stalking. It was good that snow have fallen overnight; it filled the trenches and they had to be cleared, so there were few soldiers around – just the sentries and snow-sweepers. None of the girls were allowed onto the front line that day, even though my partner and I were very keen to go and see whether our duelling opponent would appear again. The German sniper did not show up in the days that followed. Then the scouts said that if we hadn't killed him, we had most certainly wounded him, and that was why our sector was so fiercely shelled. Well, the scouts always knew everything!

I would like to stress that stalking is a serious business. It imposes a huge physical and psychological strain and demands maximum concentration, stamina, patience, skill and initiative. Imagine the scene: winter, cold, deep snow. And the sniper lies in no-man's land from dawn to dusk, between her own trenches and those of the enemy, unable to move, lest she give herself away, and glued to the eye-piece of her sights in a search for her target. Even if you can't bear it any more, you can't leave; it will be detected on the other side and that will be the end of you. In summer, when the sun is beating down mercilessly, conditions are no better. All in all, I came to the conclusion based on my own experience that being a sniper is a very difficult and dangerous profession. It was while we were stalking that we were most afraid, lest we ended up being captured by the Nazis. Everyone knew that if a woman sniper were captured, she would not survive – that was the Nazi rule. But she would not be killed straight away; she would be tortured and abused. Then photographs of tormented girls would appear in German newspapers and leaflets; they were dropped on us to intimidate us.

I saw with my own eyes what the Germans did to captured girls, and others had their own stories. At a post-war veterans' reunion, I heard from one graduate of our school how one girl was dragged away by the Germans from no-man's land. As they pulled her across the snow, she shouted out: 'Girls! Shoot me! Shoot me!' Nobody would raise a finger to shoot their friend. But then they saw what the Nazis did to her and were horrified. The woman telling this story said at the time, as if in justification of her stand: 'Well, I couldn't shoot her, I just couldn't . . .' I looked at her and thought: I couldn't have done so either. Indeed, scarcely any of our girls would have dared.

We were both congratulated for fulfilment of a responsible mission and sometime later we were awarded the medal 'For Bravery'. By that time, I already had four dead Germans in my tally. My regimental mate Galya Lepyoshkina, who always knew everything, said many years later at our first reunion in 1975 that I had been recommended then for the Order of Glory (3rd Class), but somewhere along the line somebody failed to support it. This did not bother me in the least. To be honest, I have never worried about decorations, honestly believing that my service had been sufficiently noted. To this day I remain extraordinarily proud of my medals 'For Bravery'. Incidentally, unlike many other awards, this one was presented only to those who had directly taken part in combat and displayed personal courage.

This medal was presented to me in Uralsk after the war. It so happened that, following encirclement at Landsberg and hospital treatment, I ended up in a different military unit; the war was soon over, and thus my decoration did not reach me at the front. I received my second medal 'For Bravery' nine years after the war (in 1954), when I was working in Moscow as first secretary of the Frunze district committee of the Young Communist League. One day there was a call from the district enlistment office; I was subjected to lengthy and meticulous questioning as to where I had fought, what decorations I had received and what they were for. Then I was informed that for my participation in the fighting for Kőnigsberg I had once again been awarded the medal 'For Bravery'. This medal too I was unable to receive at the front. Indeed, I did not even suspect that I had won it. And yet they had sought me out so many years later! I went to the enlistment office at the set time. There were twenty-odd people gathered there who had, like me, not received their awards back then. The presentation ceremony was very solemn and moving.

On the fortieth anniversary of victory I received the Order of the Great War for the Fatherland (2nd Class) along with other veterans and on the fiftieth jubilee I was awarded the Marshal Zhukov medal. For my achievements in the workplace I was presented with the Order of the Badge of Honour and the medal 'For Valour on the Labour Front'. But nothing remains dearer to me than my medals 'For Bravery'.

While our regiment remained in defence, our life followed a more or less calm, measured course, inasmuch as this is at all possible in front-line conditions. We had normal food rations, received newspapers and letters, and found time to relax and amuse ourselves. Our favourite occupation was sledging down a hill. Its slopes faced both our side of the battle-lines and the German side. We were running a risk by sliding down this hill because the Germans quite often shelled it, especially if they noticed any movement around it. Sometimes we would end up in unpleasant and dangerous situations; one day we had to lie flat in the snow and wait until the shelling stopped. We were warned many times that our sledging could end in tears but, being young, we simply ignored these warnings. Fortunately, we got away with it.

One day a press photographer arrived at our positions. He took a lot of pictures of us in various poses, including some of us sledging, but we did not receive the promised photographs and never encountered the snaps he had taken.

In January 1945 the division went on the offensive. Our 611th Regiment was in the first echelon. Everyone realised that the war was coming to an end, that victory was not far off, and that our advance was one episode in the concluding stage of the war. Therefore, everybody was in an excited, bellicose and resolute mood.

I have by now forgotten the date when the offensive began and the chronology and sequence of events. I could of course have got hold of books, found the relevant information, and set it out clearly. However, I am not writing a history of that period of the war, but rather my own reminiscences. Therefore, I will only describe what I remember.

There was very heavy fighting in East Prussia. It has to be said that Prussia was a loyal and reliable bulwark to the Hitler regime. When we set foot on its territory and saw the estates of its *Junkers*, we were stunned: each one of them seemed like a real minor fortress. And the Prussians fought to the end. I recall that, when the war was over and the deed of surrender signed, they were still shooting at us from round corners, attics or nearby woods. This continued until we had got rid of all suspicious people in the district where our unit was located.

And so, the long-awaited offensive began. We were moving across East Prussia, fighting our way to the west, capturing towns and population centres. Constant battles, marches between locations, offensives, attacks, casualties whether wounded or dead, blood ... And so on, day after day. Everyone's feelings became blunted; at times it seemed that there would never be an end to it. I have few surviving memories of that time. I cannot now recall even the names of all the cities whose capture I was involved in – with the exception of those where the fighting was particularly heavy: Goldap, Heilsberg, Landsberg, Grunwald and Königsberg (now Kaliningrad). But for me, a rank and file soldier, there was no difference between the battles. Apart from the one at Landsberg (now Górowo Iławeckie in Poland), but that was a special case. True, some episodes from the first period of our offensive in Prussia have stuck in the memory, but more, I would say, for their day-to-day rather than their military significance. I will describe some of them.

One day we ended up on a large and, evidently in the past, very wealthy farm. In the brick house we discovered a huge cellar literally crammed with all sorts of pickles and jams. Although we had been warned not to eat anything in German houses (we were afraid of being poisoned), we could not restrain ourselves, took a few jars, opened them and ate up with pleasure. It was extraordinarily tasty. What struck me on this farm was that everything in the house was exceptionally clean – the linen tidily put away in neat piles in a cupboard was blued, starched and not just carefully but quite exquisitely darned.

It was there in Prussia that I first understood the meaning of German pedantry and accuracy, which I had heard about before the war. That is to say nothing of the order and cleanliness in their houses. I noticed how carefully the trunks of the trees along the highways were whitened. There was a war on, at any moment some irreparable damage could occur, and they were still painting the tree trunks white. However, all this did not make us less hostile towards them; rather, it produced the opposite reaction, for we had seen what these lovers of cleanliness and tidiness had wrought in our land, how pitilessly they had smashed and wiped out everything on our territory. The things we saw when we were moving through the western districts of Russia and Byelorussia in 1944!

Here is one example. On the outskirts of one city we came across a dairy factory. The Germans had not only not wrecked it; they had not even destroyed its produce. We were terribly tired, very hungry, and needed a drink of water and a wash, but we had nothing. The wells we encountered along the way turned out to be poisoned and we were forbidden to use the water from them even for washing. And now this dairy factory and, inside it, huge quantities of milk, butter and cheese. Without pausing too long to think about it, we washed in the milk, drank our fill of it, and ate sandwiches of butter and cheese. Nobody had any bread, so we had to do without it.

I remember one other incident which could have ended tragically for me. In one place my attention was drawn by a beautiful big house. I went into it out of curiosity and, in a huge hall on the ground floor, saw a group of Germans bunched round an old man sitting in an arm-chair. It was probably a family. I was about to turn and leave, when suddenly an enchanting, fair-haired, blue-eyed little boy three or four years old ran up to me. I picked him up. He was not afraid, but the faces of the adults were overcome with real horror. At that moment the door opened and the officer in charge came in. Seeing me with a German child in my arms, he turned so pale that his face acquired a sort of green tinge. Grabbing his pistol, he pointed it at me: 'Put him down immediately, or I'll shoot!' I set the boy down on the floor and covered him with my body. I stood there, not daring to move, in fear of death from a bullet fired by one of my own regiment. The officer stood for several seconds, apparently unsure what to do, then surveyed everyone in the hall with an evil glance and went out again, vigorously slamming the door. I was perplexed; I could not understand what had thrown this officer off balance. Only later did I find out that the Nazis had captured the village where his family lived and wiped them all out – his mother, father, wife and small children.

It must be said that hardly any of the civilian population remained in the areas where fighting took place; the residents had left for the west, hoping for salvation there. Their property remained unsupervised and some of our soldiers and officers took advantage of this, helped themselves to some things and posted them home. This was not forbidden, as I remember, if kept within certain limits. But as for looting, arson, rape and suchlike, which many talk and write about today, I have no such memories. I never took anything; I felt uneasy about it. One day, it is true, I could not restrain myself and took an abandoned gold woman's pocket watch with enamel on the reverse. But I lost it just the way I had found it; it was stolen from me in hospital. Another time I picked up around a hundred very beautiful postcards. I kept them for a long time, but then, in Moscow, gave them to a little girl who was really into collecting postcards.

In February our units approached Heilsberg (now Lidzbark Warmiński in Poland) and captured it. This city was a major strategic point and its capture was important for the successful implementation of the entire Heilsberg operation – one of the biggest military operations in Prussia. Marshal Georgy Zhukov wrote that the Heilsberg operation was one of the major operations of the Second World War. All those who took part in it received a personal message of gratitude from the supreme commander-in-chief, Joseph Stalin, and that did not happen all that often. Everybody was issued appropriate documents. I did not receive one because I had left the unit, spent time in hospital and then ended up in a different unit. Nobody bothered to look for me, of course. Indeed, I found about these messages only thirty years later, when I met the girls for the first time since the war. Galya Lepyoshkina brought her document with her and showed it around.

In the course of several days we had fought our way across a distance of about a hundred kilometres and we were tired and worn out. After Heilsberg we were counting on at least a small break. But it didn't happen. The order came to proceed further towards Landsberg, without a pause. Again, we hit the road. I remember one night on the march. It was completely dark, with neither moon nor stars visible. Everyone was marching in silence and all that could be heard were the scraping of feet and the heavy breathing of a huge mass of people. From time to time a halt was called, and then all the soldiers would literally collapse onto the soft snow, striving to get even just a little rest. But fifteen or twenty minutes later we would be on our feet and off again, stupefied by fatigue, lack of sleep and food, and the damp. It seemed that everything on us was soaked through: our clothes, boots, foot wrappings, mittens. At one point my consciousness switched off and I seemed to end up in a ditch. It turned out I had dropped off to sleep on the march and fallen over. I came to, feeling that I was lying on something big and hard. I switched on my torch and saw that under me was the body of a German soldier. I wanted to get up but did not have the strength. Two soldiers came up to me, seized me under the arms and pulled me up. For some time, the three of us kept moving like that, hanging on to one another.

One morning we saw a column of civilians, both young and old, travelling from west to east, towards our rear, moving towards us in an endless stream. Among them were many men. The line of huge gypsy-style covered waggons was drawn by draught horses, a special breed I had only seen in Germany.

We had encountered streams of people like this before. They had been liberated from German captivity – Russians and Ukrainians, Poles and Yugoslavs, French and Italians, and citizens of other European countries who had been deported against their will to Germany, where they were exploited as forced labour. They also included Germans who had abandoned their houses in fear of Russian soldiers, but were now, as the war came to an end, heading back home again. To tell the truth, I had never seen such a huge mass of people, and with such a wealth of baggage.

I cannot vouch for the authenticity of what I heard later, but one regimental comrade said that some Italian had told one of our officers that there were quite a few German soldiers in the moving column and that they had weapons in the carts. What happened subsequently I have no idea, but our column went on its way and the other one did the same, heading towards our rear . . .

Heavy and extended fighting erupted on the approaches to Landsberg and we suffered major losses. But the city was taken.

A short break ensued. Soldiers were given a chance to relax.

As I remember, many of the houses in the city we captured contained crates of schnapps. Whether that was just by chance or deliberate I don't know. But our soldiers paid due respect to this drink, marking the victory that had been won at such heavy cost. One of the commanders advised us: 'Keep out of sight, girls, or our sozzled soldiers will give you no peace.'

That is what we did. Selecting a small farm several hundred metres from the town, we set off there with the intention to relaxing a bit, having a sleep and tidying ourselves up. We settled in comfortably, spread the quilts or thick down blankets on the floor, and lay down. In accordance with front-line practice, we did not undress or take off our boots, and we kept our rifles at hand. We had a snack and decided to nod off for a while. I don't know how much time had gone by; it seemed to me that I had only just shut my eyes. But suddenly I heard a heart-rending cry: 'Wake up, girls! Germans!'

How fortunate that one of the girls had had to go outside. She went out, happened to look around the fields, and saw a solid line of Germans heading towards the town. The farm in which we had so cosily accommodated ourselves was right in their path.

It turned out that our units had quietly gone off without a shot being fired. They had simply forgotten about us. We grabbed our rifles and tore off together through the gates. Around us lay flat fields; we were clearly visible from all sides. We ran straight across a marsh of soggy spring mud. Then we encountered barbed wire, could not get around it, and tried to crawl under the barbs. We managed it (though later, when the fighting was over we tried to repeat the trick and it didn't come off). We were being fired at from two sides – from both the Germans and our own soldiers, who did not know that the farm was occupied by their own troops and therefore initially took us for Germans.

We ran out onto the highway. A burst of machine-gun fire resounded from the direction of the Germans and one of the girls was wounded in the leg. We were in despair. What were we to do? We realised that she wouldn't be able to make it and we couldn't carry her. Fortunately, at that moment a cart, with a horse in harness that was demented from the fiery racket, appeared from somewhere. The woman driver standing in the cart was shouting something in horror and mercilessly lashing the horse with a whip. It was only by a miracle that we managed to stop the horse, which was charging at full speed. We loaded the wounded girl onto the cart and ran on further ourselves.

At one point I discovered that I had no one beside me; I was all by myself. I carried on running. I caught sight of a house standing on its own. Without thinking I dashed through its yard to shorten the distance. In the yard I noticed some iron crates of cartridges scattered around and automatically stuffed my pockets with them. I ran on further. I was running and bullets were whistling around me from all sides. It seemed to me as if the bullets were flying straight at me, that I was an open target. Then suddenly I felt that I could not run any further; my heart was thumping somewhere in my throat, my breathing was laboured, and my legs had turned to cotton wool. I was overcome by a feeling of complete indifference. I slung my rifle on my back and walked on. I was not frightened at the time; that came later. Suddenly I heard a call: 'They'll kill you, girl. Come over here.' I looked, and there was a trench and in it a middle-aged soldier. I jumped into the trench. Here, alongside an unknown soldier, I set about beating off the first German attack.

But what had happened to the other girls? During one of our reunions Milya Dogadkina had said that she had ended up with some tank squad or self-propelled artillery unit and repelled the Nazi attack along with them. But here is what Galya Lepyoshkina (now Dzhulai) recalls in a letter she recently sent to me:

> We dropped everything and ran out of the house. We looked round. A line of Germans was approaching. We ran out onto the roadway. Some officer with a revolver

stopped us and ordered us to take up a defensive position in the ditch. When the attack was repelled, we went back to the house and discovered on the staircase to the attic that Dusya Philipova had been savagely tortured by the Nazis . . . They had no mercy for women snipers.

Yes, they were terrible days, being encircled at Landsberg. We were in the cellar of a cheese factory, with gunners beside us. In one corner there were horses and in another one we sat on the hay. I remember Ivan Ivanovich [Popletyeyev, regimental chief of staff] tugging us by the legs when we thrust our heads out. And there was a German sniper in the factory chimney taking pot-shots at us. Then somebody 'removed' him and things became easier. I don't recall where our defensive positions were at night (in the same place, I think) and we stood in pairs with our rifles at intervals of 25 metres. It was scary! You look around, your eyes grow weary, and you imagine the Germans will creep up and grab you.

Nobody could remember later how we ended up in different locations. One can only suppose that, having run out of the house, we fanned out across the field, intuitively realising that in this way it would be easier to protect ourselves against solid fire, and we all moved in different directions. But how Dusya finished up in the clutches of the Nazis no one could say.

In the evening of the same day I was standing on the main street of the town together with the regimental commissar. We were observing enemy rockets flying up from three sides beyond the town, illuminating everything around. The commissar then told me that a train of carts was being organised to remove the wounded; it would be departing at night and needed a convoy. 'Go with them.' he suggested. 'Maybe you'll survive that way.' But I didn't go. I was afraid to tear myself away from my own comrades. And that is what saved me.

What happened subsequently shook everyone. A feature article later appeared in *Pravda* written by Alexander Tvardovsky, who was at that time a correspondent for the front-line paper *Red Army Pravda*. The article described in detail the bloody history of what took place at Grunwald. This is what happened.

The divisional hospital (Medical Battalion No. 288), where the wounded from our sector of the front were taken, was located in a huge mansion in Grunwald. The Germans, who were now in our rear, ended up at the hospital. They could see that it was a hospital in front of them; flying over the building was a white flag with a red cross on it. However, they first opened fire at it from self-propelled artillery, and then began an assault on it. The doctors, nurses, orderlies, patients – anyone who could hold a weapon – fired back, right to the end. They all perished. At the very beginning of the fighting the medics had transferred some of the seriously wounded soldiers to the cellar, so they would not suffer from the shelling. Evidently guessing that there was somebody in the cellar, the Germans drove the self-propelled vehicles up close to the building and began to pump exhaust gases into the cellar. Everyone down there suffocated from the gases with the exception of one man, who survived by a miracle. His story and surviving documents from the ruins of the hospital make it possible to re-create a picture of the tragedy. Subsequently we saw what the Nazis had done to our soldiers. We saw one girl whom they had savagely abused and tortured, and then left outside in her torn clothing on the marble steps leading to the palace. It was there in Grunwald that the string of carts which I was invited to accompany was completely wiped out. Fate protected me.

In recent years our politicians, journalists and defenders of human rights have enjoyed talking about the brutality of Soviet soldiers during the war years; some are even demanding that we apologise to the German people. War is by its very nature unnatural and brutal; it is not waged in kid gloves. As for the particular brutality of our own soldiers, I am compelled to relate some facts.

There were over 1,500 wounded German soldiers and officers left behind in Landsberg when it was occupied by our division; they were either forgotten or had not been able to be evacuated. So, what happened to them? I will cite fragments from diary entries made during the battle at Landsberg by the head of the medical-evacuation squad of the army health section, P. Vorontsov. These jottings were published in a collection of reminiscences by veterans of the 88th Division. Here is what he wrote:

> At Landsberg the Nazis abandoned 1,770 of their wounded soldiers and officers. The army health section assigned a mobile field surgical hospital and some emergency surgical groups to treat the wounded. Furthermore, the troops of the 88th Rifle Division handed the dry rations they had received for two days of fighting over to the wounded servicemen and residents of Landsberg.

One more note from the same source:

> In Landsberg soldiers of the division whose medical battalion had been wiped out discovered some German residents in a church. When they saw that they were women, old people and children, they took some bread from the hospital kitchen and gave it to them.

I stress that these are not just somebody's subjective recollections, but the diary entries of officer Vorontsov, who took part in the events. And all this was done after we found out about the Nazi atrocities at Grunwald. I particularly want to draw attention to the fact that, being encircled at the time, we were also suffering from a lack of foodstuffs. But nobody voiced displeasure at the decision to give part of our supplies to the wounded German soldiers and officers.

And this is only one of many similar examples which I happened to witness. I saw other things too: our soldiers feeding German children and old folk – frightened, hungry, and sick – in cities we captured.

I crossed the whole of Prussia with my division. I remember how, before setting foot on its territory, we were lined up and read an order which threatened the most severe punishments, even including a firing squad, for looting or taking the law into our own hands. Not once did I see our soldiers abusing peaceful civilians or prisoners of war, shooting or hanging them, wiping out whole population centres along with the old people, women and children living in them, as the Nazis had done. We did not set up concentration camps on occupied territory and did not burn people in ovens, nor did we take children from their mothers or turn them into slaves. Indeed, after what the Nazis wrought on our land, one can only marvel at the restraint of our soldiers. I knew many soldiers and officers whose families, relatives and others close to them had suffered at the hands of the Nazis. In some cases, people were shot; in others, they were exploited as forced labour, while others still remained without a roof over their heads because the Nazis had burnt everything. Nevertheless, our soldiers bore no resemblance to the Nazis. Of course, there were cases of unjustified brutality, but they were isolated cases and not systematic – unlike the Nazis, who waged war to annihilate everybody and everything. Even before the war Hitler had openly declared: 'We must develop the technique of depopulation. If you ask me what I mean by depopulation, I will tell you that I mean the removal of entire racial units, and that is what I intend to accomplish; this, bluntly speaking, is my objective . . . I have the right to remove millions of the lower races.'

This plan was implemented with particular brutality in our country. The figures are well known: it is estimated that our civilian losses were twice as high as our military losses.

Judgment on the deeds of the German Fascists was passed by the international tribunal that sat in Nuremberg from the end of 1945. Speaking at this trial, the chief prosecutor from the USA, Robert Jackson, who could in no way be accused of sympathy for the Soviet Union and its leaders, declared in his opening statement: 'Our evidence will be horrifying, and you will accuse me of disturbing your sleep. But it is these actions which made the whole world tremble . . . Germany became one vast torture chamber. The cries of their victims were audible to the world and made all civilised humanity shudder.'

The international tribunal condemned the Nazi ringleaders to the ultimate measure of the law.

On that night when, in a desire to save my life, the commissar almost sent me to certain death, the Germans completed their encirclement and we were solidly ringed in. This town occupied a special position as the endpoint of many important highways and therefore the Germans strove in every way possible to regain it. We were faced with the task of holding on to Landsberg.

This marked the beginning of heavy fighting with huge losses on both sides. We remained encircled for nine days and the bloody slaughter did not let up for a single day. On some days we had to beat off six or eight German attacks. The trenches were manned by anyone capable of holding a weapon: medics, quartermasters, soldiers from the provisions platoon, and even those who were wounded, shell-shocked or sick. The gunners dragged their artillery up to the forward line and hit the Germans over open sights, at point-blank range and, when they had fired their last shells, they came back to the trenches.

That year spring came early in Prussia. There were puddles everywhere and the trenches were also full of water. We went around wet, frozen and hungry. For days at a time we would not leave the trenches. The rations were very meagre and we basically ate the cold, dry food where we stood. At night the lads would crawl out to the field between our trenches and the German ones and bring back 'treats' like frozen potatoes. From time to time we went in small groups to the town to warm up, sleep a little and eat something hot.

My turn came around and I took great pleasure in drying off, getting warm and having a meal. Under the impact of our nightmarish conditions, I decided to write a letter to Auntie Nastassia in Moscow. I sat down right on the floor and began to write. I wrote a lot of nonsense, in particular, that I didn't want to die at the age of nineteen, that I cursed the day I was born, and other such stuff. I was sure that this letter would not get through the encirclement and simply felt like pouring out my heart and relieving the accumulation of pain and despair. But after the encirclement was breached somebody gathered up all the letters and sent them to their destinations. Whether he did this out of a sense of duty, or he was a kind man who realised that some of these letters would be, for some people, the last news from the front, from a soldier who was still alive yesterday but gone today, nobody knows. The important point is that the letters were sent to their addressees. And my letter of despair reached Auntie Nastassia, and then its contents somehow became known to my mother.

When I returned home, it was a long time before mum even indicated that she knew about the letter. Only many years later, when I suddenly recalled the encirclement, did mum ask: 'Didn't you curse the day when you volunteered for the army?' At the time I did not reply to my mother. But now I can say with total sincerity that I did not curse that day. Rather, I felt that, once I was born, I had to fulfil my destiny.

Auntie Nastassia kept that letter for a long time after the war and, when as a student I visited that small room in a communal flat on the Pervyy Kazachiy Pereulok ('First Cossack Lane'), she would gather the neighbours, bring the letter out from somewhere, and read it. Everyone would sob. I got fed up with it. One day, along with Auntie Nastassia's niece, who was staying with her at the time, I found and burnt that horrible letter. How Auntie Nastassia wept and cursed! I had never seen her so angry. But that was later.

While we were in encirclement, we did not think about what would happen next. For the moment the main thing was to stand firm. As before, we stoutly repelled all attempts by the enemy to regain the town, although that was becoming harder and harder to do.

Nevertheless, after a while I was lucky enough to enjoy another break. I went into the town with several of our girls. We were taken to an enormous, beautiful palace, which had by some miracle survived the hellish conditions. We ended up in a large hall, painted white, with a moulded ceiling and white gilded doors. Visible before us was a whole suite of rooms with their doors wide open. Some heavenly music could be heard from somewhere; it was one of our officers playing the piano.

It was warm inside. Next to one window in the hall was a large divan with a high back, while, positioned diagonally across one corner, stood some tables on which some tanks and pans gave out a tasty smell. I was hungry, but the sensation of hunger was vanquished by another desire – to lie down and sleep. I settled down as comfortably as I could on the divan in the hope of a snooze, but it was not to be. The girls shook me and urged me to eat up, as nobody could tell when we would next get soup. I resisted and kept saying: 'Sleep. I want to sleep.' Then they grabbed me under the arms, lifted me up off the divan and took me to the corner of the room and the steaming pots and pans. Suddenly, right under the window, the very one where my chosen divan stood, a shell exploded with a crash and window glass smashed and flew in all directions. Something struck me hard beneath the right knee. I looked around to see who was responsible for this stupid joke and saw with horror that the back of the divan on which I had only just been sitting so comfortably was in smithereens. I felt under my knee; my fingers brushed against something small and very hard. I fiddled around a bit inside my wadded trousers and pulled out a tiny shard. It had struck with its flat edge and got stuck in the wadding. True, the heavy blow led to acute inflammation, but that came later and, in the meantime, I rejoiced at my escape and thanked the girls who had actually saved my life. Once again fate had treated me mercifully.

There would be a number of other occasions when some such force would save me.

One day I was firing from the second floor of a house on a low hill. I had unleashed one burst of fire and quickly changed positions. I had only just settled down by a different window when a shell exploded where I had been standing just a few moments earlier and made a huge hole in the wall. What would have become of me had I disregarded our iron rule: take a shot and move on?

Another example: I was walked along a highway one day when I heard a shell whistling. From the sound I determined that it was a heavy shell and flying in my direction, seemingly right at me. I flung myself onto the ground and covered my head with my arms. I heard the shell plonk down heavily behind me, quite close by. I lay there thinking in horror: it's going to explode any minute! But it didn't explode! To satisfy their interest, the sappers later decided to see why the shell had not exploded, opened it up and there found a note: 'We help where we can.' Who was this friendly party? A Soviet citizen forced at machine-gun point to work in a German factory, or a German anti-fascist helping us out of ideological considerations? We had been aware of cases like this earlier, but this was the first time I had seen it with my own eyes. And whoever they were, whoever did it, they were risking their own lives for the sake of our salvation.

But the regiment was still encircled. For days on end we did not leave our trenches. The Germans were attacking several times a day. The situation was becoming unbelievably grave. Our supplies of provisions and ammunition were exhausted and we were sustaining serious losses. We tried to break out of the encirclement, but unsuccessfully. Several times we heard fierce shooting from the left flank. According to reconnaissance information, it was from units of the Second Byelorussian Front trying to help us and break through the ring on their side. This did not succeed either. Everyone realised that we could not hold out for long. During those days we had everyone who could possibly shoot engaged in the trenches. Even the gunners, who had run out of shells, joined the infantry in the trenches and went into the attack alongside them.

There was one moment when the soldiers had gone into yet another attack, that I looked around and realised that there was nobody in the trenches, that my comrades were all out there and I was on my own, all alone as far as I could see. I was seized by such horror that I crawled out of the trench too, caught up with the ranks, and went into the attack with them. Because sniper rifles had no bayonets, I decided to use mine like a club – on the off chance that I would be forgiven for wrecking it. Fortunately, one soldier saw me running with the others and shouted: 'Where do you think you're going, you fool? They'll kill you.' And pushed me into a nearby trench. This attack of ours also conked out

Testimony to the gravity of the environment is provided by an episode which Anya Vereshchagina reminded me of. We were approached by a quite youthful junior lieutenant – worn out, unshaven, covered with clay, and clad in an overcoat with part of its flap torn off. 'Girls,' he appealed to us, 'we're down to one soldier for every ten metres. Help us out.'

We quietly got up, took our rifles, and followed him. Back into the damp, cold trenches. And suddenly, Vera Samarina, a frail red-head, who had had a panic fear of rifles and shooting at the start of our training, climbed onto the parapet and shouted out in her feeble little voice: 'Let's get ourselves into gear, stand up to the Nazis and drive them back!' We all brightened up and got our act together. And stood up to them. We repelled the next Nazi attack.

Many soldiers subsequently carried the wounded from the field of battle along with the medics. I was also called on to help. I was crawling across a field. I heard someone calling out faintly on one side, as if crying for help. It seemed to me it was not a Russian, possibly even one of us from Kazakhstan. I crawled up and saw that lying there was a quite youthful soldier, and he really did have an Asiatic look about him. I grabbed him and began to pull him along. He was of short stature, but turned out to be incredibly heavy. I was barely able to drag him to the trench, where some soldiers helped to lower him carefully in. Suddenly he opened his eyes, felt himself with his hands and exclaimed in joy: 'I'm still in one piece!' The lad had seemingly been awfully scared. I was ready at that moment to finish him off.

We were absolutely worn out, exhausted by hunger, cold, and the damp that penetrated right through us. And then came the day when there were hardly any more cartridges or hand-grenades – just a handful each. I put two of my cartridges in my pocket – in case of emergency, so I would not fall into the Germans' clutches. We feared capture worse than death; we had seen a number of times what the Nazis did with captives.

One day, when it was beginning to get dark, a soldier came up to me and said that we would be making a break-through at night. 'Do you know what that is?'

'No, I don't.'

'It's very simple: you take your rifle, raise it above your head, and run shouting "Hurrah!" If you get through, you're lucky, if not . . . but don't worry,' he added, 'I'll get you out, even if I perish myself.'

Thus, completely by accident, in such tragic circumstances, I found out that I had an admirer. But he was twenty-seven and to me, at nineteen, he seemed an old man, so no romance eventuated.

We did not manage to break through ourselves. After a powerful 'softening up' artillery blast, which we listened to with such hope, the units of the 2nd Byelorussian Front nevertheless broke through to our area, bursting the blockade open. What a to-do there was! We hugged one another, wept and laughed, upended the soldiers who had come to our aid and thereby saved the lives of hundreds of my regimental mates. And how many of the soldiers who so stubbornly strove to break through to us lost their lives! Victory never came easy.

We then remained on defence for several days until our places were taken by fresh units. And finally, it was all over!

We abandoned the trenches. There were not many of us left. The officer in charge of our defence sector emotionally declared with tears in his eyes: 'I brought almost four hundred troops here. And now . . .' And now the number who walked away without a scratch from the forward line which we had defended for nine days was of the order of ten or fifteen. The rest were wounded, shell-shocked, sneezing with cold, or sick. And many had been killed. I was among the few lucky ones; I emerged from those many hellish days alive and well.

I don't recall where these frightful figures came from – ten to fifteen troops – or how reliable they are, but these figures have remained stuck in my memory like a splinter throughout the post-war years.

We marched to Landsberg dead tired, covered in mud and blood, dreaming only of one thing – rest. We anticipated washing the caked mud off, eating our fill and sleeping for a day or two. But quite unexpectedly for us everything turned out differently. A great many wounded had accumulated in the town because of the impossibility of evacuating them. There were not enough medical personnel and therefore we girls were required to look after the wounded. We were all sent to various medical centres; there were several in the town.

When I first came to the former church where a hospital containing 300 wounded had been set up, I felt queasy. The wounded lay in rows on straw which had been spread around the floor. The air was filled with the stench of blood, putre-faction, excrement and mouldy straw. All the wounded were being looked after by a single man, a military doctor; the other medics were with us, fighting on the front line. They carried the wounded from the field of battle, bandaged them up, administered first aid to those in the trenches and, at critical moments, took up weapons themselves and fired to repel the Nazi attacks. The military doctor had been coping alone in the hospital all these days. I do not remember the title or name of this remarkable doctor, who went for days without sleep, striving to ease the sufferings of the wounded, even just a little. But what could one man do without helpers, without bandaging material and medical supplies? Therefore, he was very pleased when we were placed at his disposal. I don't remember exactly, but I think some medics came with us; we would not have coped without them.

We did everything: fed the wounded and helped them to drink, assisted with bandaging, wrote letters for them, tidied up. One day I noticed a middle-aged soldier who kept asking for a drink. I wanted to give him some water, but the doctor forbade it – the soldier was wounded in the stomach and with a wound like that one cannot drink. I went up to him, sat down on the floor beside him, placed this unfortunate man's head on my knee and began to wet his lips with water. I remember, he would open his eyes and close them again, as he did not even have the strength to restrain his eyelids, and kept begging: 'Drink, sister.' He died like that in my arms.

I began to feel nauseous from the unbelievable smells pervading the air and the constant sight of bleeding and suppurating wounds. 'Have a smoke, and you'll find it easier,' the doctor said. We began to smoke. For the majority it did not become habitual, but some took to it and smoked for the rest of their lives.

Here too are some recollections from Galya Lepyoshkina, who was working at this time in a different place, in a field hospital that had only just been set up:

> I was working with a surgeon ... The wounded were coming in from the front line ... The doctor made me hold the foot of a wounded man during an operation on his heel ... We were young ... What did we understand? The wounded were naked; I was embarrassed and turned away. I was at the limit of my endurance. The wounded man was screaming, and the doctor demanding: 'Hold on!' Just to remember that dirt and the blood ... And besides that, we were not medical orderlies, but we did everything ... For four days we were unable to eat or drink. The main thing was going without sleep. We very nearly croaked ourselves!

At last came the happy moment when we loaded the last of the wounded onto trucks and sent them to the rear. The time had come for us to leave Landsberg. Galya was right; we could barely stand on our own feet and looked no better than those we had been taking care of all these days. We were sent to a reserve battalion for rest and re-formation. I don't recall how we got there, but it was most likely on foot. I remember marching through a wood on the outskirts. Here we unexpectedly stumbled across the body of a captain, the commander of surveillance forces and a good friend of ours. He was lying under a tree, half covered by soft dirty snow. The Germans had broken his legs and then shot him point-blank; his face showed burns and traces of powder. We placed the captain's body on the cart and carried it off, walking beside it. I could not tear my eyes away from his fair hair, which fluttered in the breeze, as if he were still living. It seemed that the hair was alive on its own, independent of the immobile dead man. It was a troubling sensation. The body was carried off to the rear and buried there.

We joined a reserve regiment. Again, the same old double-layered bunks, and, on them, my long-suffering and far from well regimental mates, who had become so close and dear to me. We made up for lost sleep and hunger, treated our ailments, rested, and put our uniforms and weapons in order. The unit was replenished with fresh soldiers and officers.

These days, when so many years have gone by, I try to recall or even to imagine what my friends and I endured, living through the nightmare of encirclement. The main sensation was of course huge joy at remaining alive but, as well as that, weariness beyond belief. It seemed to me that what we had lived through was beyond the bounds of human ability to cope. Soldiers even fought when, it would appear, there was nobody to fight and nothing to fight with. But they all held out and overcame the obstacles, nor did they waver or give in. No doubt there were cowards and panic-merchants among us, but I don't remember this. The main thing I recall is the courage and staunchness with which the soldiers fought, what powers of endurance they showed, and how they supported and helped one another. This I remember.

My admiration for our girls has lasted to this day. They really were still girls in terms of age and life experience, but in an unbelievably difficult and dangerous environment they held together in a worthy fashion; nobody wavered or took a backward step, or attempted to hide behind the backs of others and save her own life at their expense.

Our stay in the reserve regiment was coming to an end, when that tiny bit of metal which ended up under my knee-cap started to play up. I began to suffer from inflammation of the right knee joint. I could not even walk from the pain. I was sent to a medical centre and from there to one hospital, then to another. I said goodbye to the girls before I left. I hoped to return to my unit after treatment and did not imagine that I would be faced with fighting on one front while they were on a different one. My war finished at Königsberg and theirs near Prague. What bothered me most back then was that I was on my own, without my faithful friends. Nobody imagined that we would only meet again thirty years later . . .

I recall being driven to the hospital in a small ambulance. It was cold on board and I lay on a stretcher hanging from the ceiling in my overcoat, boots and winter cap. My sore leg was dreadfully frozen and my cap kept creeping down over my face. I would straighten it up, but it would creep down again. When I took it off, my head got cold, so I put it back on again. The ambulance was shaking violently on the bumpy roads, the stretcher swung from side to side and, by the end of the journey, I felt quite unwell from the shaking and the awful pain in my leg. Finally, we arrived. The medical orderlies, quite young girls of roughly my own age, laid me on a stretcher and carried me up to the third floor and the reception area. It was apparent how hard it was for these girls to carry me, but by that time I could not walk at all and I was also quite shaken up. I would not have been able to get up to the third floor. Following a doctor's examination, I had a hot bath. The middle-aged orderly who eagerly washed the many days of trench muck off me kept intoning a quiet lamentation: 'Dear Lord . . . and still a child . . . ribs sticking out . . . like someone out of a concentration camp . . . What have they done to you . . . the devils.' I completely relaxed from the warm water and the soft sound of the orderly's voice, my eyes kept closing and it even became hard to move. After the bath I was clad in clean linen and put in a clean bed. What bliss! For the first time in several months – hot water, fresh linen, a pillow, sheets! I was warm and dry, with hot food three times a day. And peace and quiet, no shooting. At first, I felt odd in this silence and imagined that it would be followed by some dreadful event. Left alone among strangers, I suffered a lot and pined for my friends in the regiment. Besides that, while I was in the medical centre, I was constantly pursued by the fear of possible encirclement – a repetition of what had happened to the 288th Medical Battalion, destroyed by the Nazis. Most of all I was afraid of being left unarmed. I had to surrender my rifle and I had grown so close to it that I felt defenceless without it. 'What if the Germans reach the medical centre? How will I defend myself?' I often thought. Then I began to get concerned about my leg. In the first hospital amputation had been suggested because the infection had gone very deep. I naturally refused. Then I was sent to another hospital, where the surgeon said that only a complete ignoramus and surgical amateur would have proposed such a stupid thing.

Nevertheless, he could not see any point in treatment with medicine and I was faced with an operation, so I ended up in the operating theatre. I managed to note that it was a huge hall filled with a multitude of tables where my fellow soldiers were under the knife. I was laid on a table. I looked one way, where something was bleeding. I looked in another direction, and there, on a table, lay a quite young lad. The whole side of his body that was visible to me had been slashed, as if with knives, by mortar splinters. The wounded groaned, and screamed, and swore obscenities. The surgeon bent over me. 'I'm sorry, but I'll be operating without anaesthetic,' he 'greeted' me. 'We haven't enough for more serious operations. So, you'll have to put up with it.' And he proceeded to cut into my live flesh. This was the second time I had been under the knife with no anaesthetic. The pain was unbearable. I didn't think I could hold out, that I would begin screaming. But I gripped the edge of the table with both hands, gritted my teeth, screwed up my eyes, and held out.

Next morning my neighbours in the ward said I had groaned during the night, cried out dreadfully and struggled to escape. It seemed to them I was having a bad dream, but they did not attempt to wake me. That was a pity. Already then, I had begun to be tormented by nightmares about capture and encirclement. These dreams pursued me for a long, long time after the war. It was only after I had met the other girls thirty years later that these dreams became less frequent, and then, fortunately, they almost completely disappeared from my life.

There were five or six of us in the ward. One of them has stuck in my memory. She was a civilian who worked in the baths and laundry detachment. One day she had carelessly tipped a tub of boiling water over herself. Her legs were badly scalded. She lay on the bed next to mine and on top of her was a wire frame covered with cheese cloth, because it was impossible to cover her with anything else. Only once did I see how her legs had suffered. After that I turned away when a doctor or nurse came to treat that bloody mess. And when any of us passed her bed, she would pucker up her face because even the slightest vibration of the floor caused her unbelievable pain. We were all back then staggered by this woman's courage, patience and powers of endurance and strove to disturb her as little as possible.

After the operation I was treated with some medicines, ointments and paraffin lozenges. Everything healed.

From the hospital I again ended up in a reserve regiment, but a different one. Here I was on my own – not a single familiar face; all strangers. I remember attending some exercises and waiting for a new assignment. There was no possibility of going back to my own regiment or even to my own division; they were fighting on a different front.

One day the regimental command turned to those of us who were in the reserve regiment; fierce battles were raging at the front and blood was needed for the wounded. Many took off immediately to give blood and, of course, I did too. When I arrived they dressed me in all white garments, even some ragged white socks for my feet. I was sat down on a high couch. But somehow things did not work out for the nurse. She had only just begun to drain the blood when the needle jumped out of the vein and blood streamed onto the floor. The nurse was nervous and could not connect with the vein, while the blood kept flowing out. I lost a lot of blood and got up from the couch feeling drunk. All the donors were then taken to the mess hall and given some vodka and a nice dinner. I went back to the barracks satiated, very happy and extremely merry. I was noisy and merry for a long time, till I dropped off to sleep on my bunk, still in my clothes.

Finally, an order came: I was assigned to the Alexander Nevsky Howitzer Regiment under the high command reserve. But what was a sniper like me to do in an artillery regiment? Maybe there had been no requests for snipers. Possibly the person who decided my fate did not even know that I was a sniper. Or perhaps fate was still showing concern for me?

It was useless to speculate, or to object to the secondment. You were not supposed to do that. Orders were to be fulfilled to the letter – I had understood that back at sniper school. I gathered up my meagre soldier's kit, put it in a bag along with some dry rations, and headed off to an artillery regiment which was unfamiliar to me. I got there on foot with occasional lifts from vehicles along the way. By night time I had reached the regimental staff headquarters and from there I was taken to a battalion led by Captain G., a coarse and unscrupulous man, it later turned out, with a fondness for wine and women. At the same time, he had the reputation of being an excellent, organised and bold commander, for which much was forgiven him.

Unfortunately, on the night I joined the battalion he was, to put it mildly, under the influence and still awake when my arrival was announced. At this time the battalion was being put up for the night somewhere. The administration platoon to which I was being seconded occupied a room in a house which I was not able to view clearly in the dark. And in the next room was my future commanding officer, diverting himself with a bottle. In complete darkness and accompanied by a sentry, I went through to my platoon's room and stopped in hesitation. By the meagre light of a kerosene lamp I saw some soldiers sleeping higgledy-piggledy on the floor, and so close together that there was nowhere to step. The sentry struggled to step over the soldiers and got through to a corner of the room. I followed him. Then the soldier accompanying me roughly pushed aside somebody sleeping on the only bed in the place and offered me his place. I stood there, not daring to take this step. 'Don't worry,' said the soldier, 'they're great lads. They won't bother you.' Eventually I lay down on the bed – like the others, without undressing. However, I did not manage any sleep. An orderly soon arrived from the captain.

'The captain wants to see you.'

'I'm not going.'

'What do you mean, not going? They'll court-martial you for insubordination.'

'Let them. I'm still not going.'

By that time, I had heard enough stories of some officers' amorous advances, tricks perpetrated on girls, and those women who were contemptuously known as 'campaign wives'. In my old regiment, No. 611, there was none of this; the commanders them-selves treated us with caution and would not allow other officers to take liberties. Besides, there were a number of girls there, but here I was the only one. I didn't know anybody at all here; I was defenceless and therefore scared.

The orderly left, then came back with the same message: the captain wanted to see me. The third time he came back with orders to take me there, at rifle-point if necessary. I couldn't do anything. I got up and went with a sinking heart. As we passed through the small, dark lobby my escort warned me.

'Be careful. The captain's drunk.'

'Don't leave, please. Stand by the door while I'm with him.'

He duly stayed and I stepped into the room, raising my hand to my cap.

'Comrade Captain, Junior Sergeant Zhukova at your command.'

He sat me on a chair and poured me a glass of vodka without any preliminaries.

'Drink!'

'I don't drink, Comrade Captain.'

'Drink, I said!'

'I don't drink.'

'What, you don't drink at all?'

'Not at all.'

'Well, to hell with you!' and he wobbled drunkenly on his chair.

This was followed by a scene which I have no wish to describe. In essence, taking advantage of the fact that he was drunk and barely able to stand on his feet, I slipped away. The orderly was waiting for me outside. He calmed me down as best he could and took me back to my bed. As I entered the room, I was amazed; the lamp was burning bright as bright, the soldiers were no longer asleep, and they were all looking at me. The orderly muttered something softly to them, I suddenly saw smiles light up the faces of some soldiers, and one of them said quietly: 'Well done, girl!' Within a minute the room once again resounded with the powerful snores of my new comrades. The soldier turned out to be right; the lads in the platoon were a splendid lot and three of them subsequently became true 'knights in shining armour' and reliable protectors to me. They were all slightly in love with me. I remember each of them well.

Senior Sergeant Vasily Stolbov was my immediate superior. Tall, a little stooped, and reserved, with a slightly husky voice, he always took a cautious attitude towards me. He never spoke about his feelings with me and it was only after the war, when I was returning home, that he sent two letters in one envelope – for my mother and me – and declared his love for the first time. But it is to him that I am indebted for the warm, friendly relations I had with all the lads in the platoon. He never allowed anyone to upset me by taking liberties, harassment, or insinuations.

Alexei Popov was a tall, statuesque and very attractive man and his appearance was much enhanced by his broad open smile. He was incidentally the only one in the battalion (perhaps the only one in the regiment) to take part in the victory parade on 24 June 1945, on Red Square in Moscow. Alexei was not shy about expressing his feelings and even made a marriage proposal to me, promising to divorce his wife. We had a lot of conversation on this topic. He probably said something later to his wife, because after the war I received a letter from her in which she thanked me for not taking away her husband.

Pyotr Chirkov differed markedly from Vasily and Alexei. He was a typical rustic wag – thick-set, semi-literate and always wearing a rather simple expression on his face. However, he was an outstanding and loyal friend, who was never afraid of offering me protection against anyone. When he saw one day how much the captain's coarse advances were bothering me, Pyotr told him straight to his face: 'Leave Junior Sergeant Zhukova in peace. I love her, she loves me, and after the war we have decided to cement our love in marriage.' After that poor Pyotr was eternally on the lists for extra duties. And one day he rudely told me in passing: 'I curse the day when we got landed with you.' The lad was at his wit's end!

But in relations between us nothing changed. Every time I appeared in our overwhelmingly male company, Pyotr would strike up loudly, at the top of his voice: 'In the days when I drove the postal waggon . . .', a dismal ditty about an ill-starred love affair. Given his complete absence of a singing voice or an ear for music, the impact of the 'serenade' was fantastic. I always felt embarrassed in this situation, but my pleas had no effect on him and he invariably greeted me with this song and a sorrowful expression on his face.

Later on, after the war, all three of them wrote to me in Uralsk. But in my desire to forget the war and everything that could remind me of it, I did not reply to a single letter. How could I have behaved like that? Besides, my efforts to reshape my memory were all in vain; I never forgot anybody or anything. If only I could turn back the clock! I would write them all long letters, choose the warmest, kindest words for them. Now I can just say one thing: 'Forgive me, lads. I always remembered you and I am grateful to fate for making you part of my life.'

It was April 1945. Our regiment was moving towards Königsberg. By order of the battalion commander I was appointed senior telephone operator. Vasily Stolbov quickly taught me all the intricacies of my new military profession. I now had in my hands a submachine gun instead of a rifle. Thank goodness we were taught at the school how to use it.

I have very vague memories of events that month. Even the fierce battles for Königsberg have left no imprint in my memory – nothing like the deep impression made by the earlier events I had to endure as part of the 611th Regiment. I did not get soaked in the trenches, I did not participate in an attack, and I was not subject to constant, unceasing fire. Or had I just got used to it? I recall the extremely powerful artillery attack which our regiment unleashed on Königsberg, the continuous deafening racket of guns and heavy mortars, solid fire, suffocating smoke. However, after Landsberg all that did not appear so frightening. It still seems to me that the infantry has it the hardest.

It has to be said that here too I was protected where possible. For this, I think, I am indebted first and foremost to our commissar, Major Yurasov. Although in 1942 the commissar's position was abolished, and instead units had deputy commanders with political responsibilities, we continued to call them commissars from habit and for the sake of brevity. And, to tell the truth, we preferred the old name – commissar. In my mind this word was associated with heroism, courage and loyalty. Our commissar was a fair man, never rude to his subordinates even at the most critical moments, and he liked the soldiers and had a protective attitude towards them.

And so it turned out that in the last month of the war, when it would have been so unlucky to lose your life, I ended up in relative safety at the battalion staff headquarters, ensuring communications between the command and the detachments.

On 9 April our forces took Königsberg. And then we were off somewhere else.

The adventures I lived through! I remember how during one lengthy and very tough march one of the soldiers offered me the chance to rest a little and ride part of the way on horseback. He brought up the horse, which was asleep on its feet, said it was very gentle, and helped me to clamber into the saddle. I had not only never ridden a horse, but never even been near one. I was not comfortable and I was about to ask for help to get down from the horse when suddenly a shell exploded close by. My 'gentle' horse took off at full speed! I must have looked very amusing and the whole line along which the horse bore me was engulfed in laughter. Then somebody finally halted the 'speedster', grabbed me and placed me on the ground. I was barely able to get my breath back.

Much more successful was my experiment with a bicycle, which I enjoyed riding for a while. On the roads we followed there was a lot of abandoned gear: cars, motorcycles and bikes in good repair, which had been left there by their owners. We enjoyed making use of them when circumstances allowed.

Often, in the fields and on the roads, we encountered stray horses and whole herds of pitifully mooing cows who had nobody to milk them; the poor animals stared at us with sad eyes. Among the soldiers there was always somebody who knew how to milk a cow and therefore we were often treated to milk fresh from the udder. Cows were also the main source of our meat supplies. We ate nothing but fresh meat.

Many sad memories remain from that period, as indeed from the war as a whole. On the march one day I saw a stack of large charred objects near a farmhouse close to the road. Unable to see from a distance what they were, I approached closer. You cannot imagine the horror that gripped me when I saw that the charred objects were actually the bodies of our soldiers. That, evidently, was how the Nazis dealt with prisoners of war. Other soldiers and officers came up, stood for a while and removed their caps. Then the commander ordered that they should all be buried and left a detail of soldiers to do this, while the rest of us went on our way. You should have seen and heard the soldiers. I was simply bawling my eyes out, not hiding my tears.

We celebrated May Day on the march, and continued marching into the night. There was no shooting to be heard. We were striding along the road and chatting. Somebody had offered me something and I was enjoying eating it on the march. Suddenly the door of the car in front, which was equipped as a communication centre, opened and somebody leaned out and shouted at the top of his voice: 'Comrades! Berlin has been taken!' 'Hurr-a-a-ah' came the powerful response. We all hugged one another; some played the accordion, while others danced there and then on the road.

'Enough! Continue the march!' sounded the voice of the commander in a joyous tone.

Over the next few days the regiment received the order to quarter itself temporarily at Geidau. This was a small place [now known as Prozorovo] not far from the Baltic Sea. We lived in anxious expectation; what would happen to us now? We knew from radio broadcasts that the war was practically over. Everyone was thinking: maybe they can do without us now. Perhaps we'll survive. We so wanted to hope that this was the case. It would be unfortunate to perish at the gates of victory.

Then came the historic day. On that memorable night, as always in battle conditions, the soldiers slept higgledy-piggledy on the floor without removing their clothes or boots, all in one room. And I was with them, my comrades. Now I was no longer afraid of them; I had dependable friends and protectors. Suddenly in my sleep I heard a soft whisper: 'Junior Sergeant, Yulia, get up. Victory has been announced.' It was Stolbov, who wanted to do me a favour and ensure I was the first to know.

But then a miracle occurred. Everyone in the room woke up from this soft whisper as if on command. There had been times when they had slept so soundly to the racket of artillery cannonades that you couldn't wake them, and yet here they had all woken up together. Seizing their weapons, they leapt outside. What ensued was something quite unimaginable: hugs, tears, laughter, disorderly shots in the air. The gunners let off several mighty volleys in the direction of the sea. An accordion appeared from somewhere and music started up, along with improvised dancing. Victory! The long-sought victory! From now on this word would be written with a big V because our Victory was a great feat on the part of the entire nation, which had paid very dearly for it. A new state celebration would be inaugurated – Victory Day

CHAPTER 7

The Sounds of Battle Die Away

If there are such things as miracles, then one of them occurred on this day, when the war ended. For many days on end we had had overcast, cold weather, with rain. But on this day the sun shone brightly, as if also celebrating our victory.

It was the beginning of a new life, a life almost peaceful. We remained in Geidau. Our choice fell on an empty two-storeyed brick house. The platoon was allotted a large room on the ground floor. We settled in and adjusted to life there. The soldiers dragged in some double-layered bedsteads from somewhere and packed the room with them. The battalion command offered me separate quarters in an altogether smaller room in the mezzanine. I refused, realising that there I would have no peace from my suitors. Subsequent experience proved me right.

So, from now on I would live in the same room as the soldiers. It wasn't easy to make this decision, but I could see no other outcome. This did not embarrass the lads in the least; they also realised I had no choice. They found me an ordinary iron single bedstead, a mattress, pillow and blanket. They put the bed in a corner, stabilised the wooden posts against the wall, and hung huge sheets over them. I now had my own 'boudoir'. Of course, I did not feel very cosy or at ease here. Say what you like, but the presence of twenty brawny young men was bound to have a restrictive effect. On the other hand, it was also a guarantee of safety, albeit in relative terms. So far as I know, none of the lads ever peeped into my corner. Perhaps there were some inclined to do so, but the others would not have allowed anyone to violate the good friendly relations between us.

Now that the fighting was over, I felt particular acutely what it was like to be alone in male company. For, besides my own lads, nearby there were many other brawny young men who had pined for female attention and tenderness over the years of war. I began to experience difficult times in a different respect, mainly psychologically and with regard to day-to-day living. At first, problems arose at literally every step. Take, for instance, the everyday question of toilets. There was one wooden toilet standing in an open place a few dozen metres from the house, and it was visible from all sides. Whenever I went there, everybody would stare, and some would call out. I could barely restrain myself from looking round, going back, or running away. I found it offensive and embarrassing, but there was no alternative. Or – another example – when they all went in formation to the Russian bath house, which had been constructed not far away, and I couldn't go with them when I desperately needed a wash. The lads guffawed and waited to see what would happen. It was just as well that Stolbov came to the rescue. 'The others will bath first, then you go, and Pyotr, Alyosha and I will keep guard.' And they duly stood guard while I was in the bath. And where was I to dry my underwear? I couldn't hang it outside for all to see.

There were very many problems like this. But little by little it was all was sorted out and things settled down. It was much harder to cope with the purely male environment, in which I was the sole object of amorous attraction. I was only nineteen and I was really bothered by endless pestering from officers. Because of them, I refused to eat in the officers' mess, to which they had admitted me by way of exception as the only woman in the detachment. I went there for two or three days, but it soon became objectionable; as I walked in, there would be dozens of male eyes fixed on me. I felt as if I was being forced to run a gauntlet. I decided to renounce my 'privileges' and began to go to the soldiers' mess. In all weathers I would stand with the lads in line, mess tin in hand, at the soldiers' mess, if indeed it could be called that. Standing in the open air were long tables knocked together from planks, benches planted in the earth, and a wooden roof overhead – such was our mess. On the other hand, when I sat down, a mountain of treats would appear before me – sweets, chocolate, biscuits – courtesy of my dear fellow soldiers spoiling me. At first, we were terribly badly fed: oatmeal porridge in the morning, oatmeal soup for dinner, more porridge and some sweet jelly made of oats, and oatmeal porridge again for supper. We felt the changes in our diet very acutely. But for the last period of our stay in Prussia the unit was responsible for its own provisioning and we dined splendidly. I have already mentioned that we were spoiled with fresh meat and milk straight from the cow. And after military operations ceased, we were put on centralised supplies. Gradually, everything came right, but for a time we lived on nothing but oats. Looking for amusement, the lads would rise from the table uttering loud harmonious neighing sounds.

But I was fighting an unequal battle with my ardent commanding officers. The casualties of this war were not only me, but my fellow servicemen as well.

One day the battalion commander, Captain G., harshly punished the entire platoon on account of my intractability. It was a trivial pretext. A feature film was being shown at the regimental HQ that evening. Naturally everyone, including me, wanted to see it. The commissar gave permission for the platoon to attend. We were escorted by one of the officers and we marched there in formation, singing. The screening finished very late and we came back all together around two o'clock in the morning. That is when the storm broke. It turned out that I had been required by the captain for some reason; they had searched for me, but not found me. And when we arrived, despite the fact that it was the middle of the night, the captain gave orders that all the bedsteads were to be removed and, in their place, double-layered wooden bunks erected. Stolbov pleaded for a bed to be left for me: 'After all, she is a girl, Comrade Captain.' But G. gruffly and spitefully replied: 'She's not a girl here, but a junior sergeant.' In this way he was reminding me of what I had once told him in response to his pestering: 'As far as you are concerned, comrade captain, I am not a girl, but a junior sergeant.' In a single night, the soldiers constructed bunks for themselves and replaced my bedstead with a wooden trestle bed. And once again I heard: 'So much trouble because of her, damn her!' I was incredibly offended but I realised that the lads had genuinely suffered on my account.

Captain G. constantly humiliated me with petty vindictiveness and fault-finding. Take, for example, this case. Serving in the battalion was an outstanding cobbler, no longer young in years. He decided to sew me some canvas boots, as the artificial leather ones were hot and heavy. The captain found out and forbade it: it was not appropriate for junior ranks. He would not allow me to replace my dreadful canvas belt with a leather one, for the same reason – not appropriate.

Everyone knew that in many units, girls were allowed some liberties when it came to uniform. Our commanding officer ostentatiously banned all of them.

Nor was that the end of the matter. It came up when I was placed on guard outside at night with other soldiers. The men would be asleep and I would be wandering around outside with a submachine gun, guarding them. My loyal 'knights' could not of course remain indifferent to this disgrace. They did not say anything to me, but I soon noticed that I had acquired a security squad. It looked amusing: I would be walking around the premises and, some distance away, one of the lads would be following, striving to camouflage himself behind the bushes or trees. Naturally, they were hiding not from me but from the officers, who would not only have banned such initiatives but could have handed out punishment for it. Fortunately, my night-time vigils did not last long. Apparently, someone made the captain realise the absurdity of the situation. Or maybe he reached that conclusion himself.

I was very much afraid that the lads would really begin to hate me. Fortunately, this did not happen. There were many occasions which convinced me that my friends were really splendid lads who understood and weighed up everything correctly. It even appeared to me sometimes that they enjoyed guarding a young girl and feeling like real protectors.

The lads took a jealous interest in my morals. I remember that G. once invited me for a ride on a motor-bike. I was afraid and would not agree for a long time, but then decided that he was not after all such a scoundrel and he couldn't upset me. And I went with him. It was a great ride. The captain rode into a forest of indescribable beauty: fresh greenery, a multitude of flowers, intoxicating scents and deafening silence. After all we had lived through it was something quite unreal. But when we got back home, my heart fell; almost the entire platoon was standing by the barracks and the lads were steadfastly watching us. Evidently, they did not detect anything suspicious and dispersed. Another time, when all the women in the regiment were taken for a medical check-up, I also detected my friends 'on guard' on my return from the medical centre. However, this time they were not looking at me, but somewhere over my head. I turned around and saw the sergeant-major accompanying me standing there with a smile on his face and giving the lads the 'thumbs up' sign.

And that was how I lived, under the constant and genuinely tiresome observation of both soldiers and officers. It was a tough life, but there was no way out.

Unfortunately, another persistent admirer appeared, the adjutant, Captain V. O. He was, it is true, a more cultivated man and he did not allow himself any liberties with regard to me. But his constant summonses really got me down. I did not have the right to refuse because he always found some task which I was obliged to perform. But as soon as I appeared in his office, a record would be placed on the gramophone of Vadim Kozin singing the romance

> I endlessly regret
> My futile predilections
> And the pain of recollections
> Weighs me down.
> I'd love to find my happiness with thee,
> But, evidently, that is not to be.

And so on.

A number of times he declared his love for me. I believed he was sincere. I also had warm feelings towards him. They were not yet love, but they were capable of becoming love. However, the captain was in a hurry and one day came out with the phrase: 'Who are you keeping yourself for? In any case nobody in civvy street will believe in your honour.' This conversation took place near a pond in which I was washing his clothes. I did washing for a lot of people, including soldiers, often washed the floors and kept the barracks tidy; there were no other women. On that occasion, I recall, I happened to be holding the captain's tunic. I took the wet garment and hit him in the face with all my might. I was instantly horrified by what I had done because I could receive a very grave punishment for insulting an officer. The captain looked at me, turned and walked away without saying anything. The incident remained unpublicised.

V. O. later apologised to me and attempted to smooth over what he had done. But I was unable to forgive his insult. I did not reply to the letter he later sent me in Uralsk. Nor did he write again. However, I kept his photograph, which had written on the back: 'Remember someday that I loved you, love you and will continue to love you, even though you did not believe me.' So ended my relations with this man. Possibly I was wrong in my harsh judgement of a man who had spent four years at war and become embittered. But what's past is past.

Demobilisation was drawing near. Around the beginning of July all the lads in our platoon were transferred to some other area and our platoon's quarters were occupied by other soldiers – those who were to be dispatched home ahead of the queue; they were getting on in years and unwell. I was retained here because I was also subject to priority demobilisation along with other women. I did not feel so comfortable sharing a room with soldiers I was unfamiliar with.

My new room-mates were languishing in boredom and inactivity as they awaited demobilisation. Their superiors decided to organise activities for them. I was appointed commander of one of the squads, put in charge of ten soldiers who were far from young and extremely weary from the war and everything that had fallen to their lot. When I lined them up the first time for activities associated with parade drill, they openly told me that they did not need this any more and had no wish to do it. I understood how they felt: indeed, what was the point of square-bashing if they would be heading home on a train within a few days? But discipline is discipline and nobody can cancel a commanding officer's orders. I too openly voiced my opinion on this matter, but added that, unless they submitted to me, it was I rather than they who would be punished. We came to terms and the exercises began. To everybody's delight, these pointless activities did not continue long.

The days till departure were numbered. But my suitors continued to trouble me. One night, Captain G. came to my room, abruptly opened the curtains by my bed and began to declare his love, proposing that I should become his wife. I was revolted by this nocturnal declaration but I was even more ashamed before the soldiers, assuming that they were not asleep and were listening to what was going on. I attempted to explain things to the captain, but it was useless; he would not listen and continued in the same vein. After the furious captain had left, one of my new middle-aged neighbours in the room, realising how unpleasant it was for me and how ashamed I was over what had happened, said: 'Come over here, girl. Don't be scared. No one will upset you here.' When my suitor came the following night, he did not find me in the usual place; I was sleeping in full uniform on a top bunk along with the soldiers.

At last the long-awaited day of departure arrived.

CHAPTER 8

Home!

I was going home. All my platoon comrades came to see me off. They spoke kind words, thrust into my hands gifts which had been captured as trophies. I didn't take anything; all those lads had mothers, sisters, wives, fiancées at home; they should be the beneficiaries of such things. It was only when the vehicle had started moving that someone leapt onto the running board and planted his forage cap on my head with the words: 'It looks really frightening on you.' I have kept the cap to this day.

But I did take some gifts – from the regimental command: about eight kilos of flour (at a time of hunger it was a truly royal gift); a German officer's overcoat of fine grey-bluish cloth (I dreamt of making an overcoat out of it, but Mum immediately sold it 'to rid the house of that obscenity'); and – from my friends – a small down pillow ('so you can sleep better along the way') and a wooden box, which they had made themselves and painted green. And I also took my own trophies – over a hundred postcards with pictures of German cities.

The truck moved off, and the lads waved to me and called out. I responded likewise, but my thoughts were already far away. I was filled with enormous joy that it was all over, but I had only one desire – to board the train as quickly as possible and get home!

However, I did not immediately get away. I had to go back to my unit a few days later. It turned out that the demobilisation documents for our whole team had been incorrectly made out and, as one of its most literate members, I was entrusted with the task of returning to the unit and checking that everything was put in order. I was given a soldier as an escort and for protection. We managed with some difficulty to get to Königsberg and spent the night for some reason in two telephone boxes close by, bedding down on some piles of paper found on the roadway. In the morning we re-joined our comrades. How delighted we all were!

Having made out the documents, we went back to the reserve regiment three days later. A few days after that it was back to the station and onto a train. Now I really was off home.

It was a long journey, I was once again on my own among a crowd of men in a huge Pullman carriage and this resulted in a lot of inconvenience. Once more, I had a spot on the bunks fenced off for me, only this time with a waterproof cape; again, my sleep was interrupted by massive male snoring intermixed with obscene language and dreadful cries during the night. The carriage could not be aired from the thick smell of shag tobacco, vodka fumes and male sweat. It was just as well that the weather was warm and the carriage door was open almost around the clock; I sat by it most of the time, enjoying the fresh air and vistas of peaceful life.

As before I was living my life in full view of men who were strangers to me. I could not wash properly, or rinse the sweat and dirt off; it was not something you would do with men watching all around. And I had a constant sensation of fear and awkwardness in the presence of men I did not know. There were problems once more over the toilet; it was a real circus. The train would stop in the steppe and an announcement would come through the loudspeaker: men to the left, women to the right. But women meant just me because I was the only one in the entire train. You looked one way and there was a mass of people; you looked in the other direction and, dashing round like a frightened hare, was just one girl searching for a hill or ditch where she could hide from hundreds of male eyes. And I would also be followed by a shout from some smart-aleck: 'Fresh air!' How many times have I thought: if only I could meet that genius who shoved a nineteen-year-old girl onto a men-only train! I would give him what for. The only comfort was the thought that I was going home.

Right throughout the journey we were met at each station by local residents, who welcomed us with music, flowers and treats. Trains of victorious troops were heading east one after another . . . and we were greeted like victors.

Everyone has probably seen news film shots of soldiers returning from the front being greeted. I struggle to hold back the tears when I watch these scenes. I see my own train, which took me to my home town of Uralsk; it was adorned with a portrait of Stalin, slogans on red banners, pine twigs and flowers. We were greeted just as rapturously at all stations by women and children; they scrutinised us with such expectation, hoping for a sight of a husband, son or father . . .

Finally, we arrived in Minsk. Here I parted without regret from my fellow-travellers. I would travel on by another train headed for Kazakhstan. I had no trouble finding the carriage I was assigned to. I walked up to it, looked in and saw girls; it was a women's carriage. What luck! I climbed up and bagged a place on the bunks. I was standing by the door, when I saw a girl forcefully pushing her way through the crowd on the platform as she made her way to our carriage. I took a closer look and recognised Roza Vozina from my own city! It is amazing how things turn out; it was here that we had parted in 1944, as we travelled to different fronts and it was here that we met again. We were both overjoyed, sat ourselves side by side on the bunks, and talked – talked without end. She incidentally said that she had heard from someone that I had been killed. Mistakes like this happened.

The track from Minsk to Uralsk seemed long and wearying. And the closer we got to home, the more excited and impatient I grew. After passing through Saratov I don't think I slept or ate, saw nothing, and did not react to anything. I had one thought in my head: to get home as fast as possible! There were moments when I felt like leaping out of the carriage and running along the sleepers, so I could, it seemed to me, get to my own home more quickly.

And then, on 6 August 1945, the train arrived in Uralsk. It slowed down and, unable to wait till it had stopped altogether, I leapt out of the carriage in my impatience and the girls handed me my rucksack and the green wooden box while the train was still moving. I stood on the platform paralysed with happiness, unable to take a single step. I did not notice anything around me. I could not believe I was home. My uniform had faded almost white, and had been pretty badly creased and stained in the course of the two-week 'journey'; my artificial leather boots were covered with dust, my forage cap was at the wrong angle, my rucksack, also faded and full of holes, on my back, my overcoat, with its burnt flap, over my left arm, and the box of gifts in my right hand.

Suddenly I heard: 'Yulia, Yulia!' I looked round and the book-keeper from mum's workplace was running towards me. Her sister had also been at the front and I assumed that she had come to meet *her*. That turned out not to be so; she had come to meet *me*. But why her? And how did it become known that I was arriving today? I had not told anyone about my arrival and wanted to keep it as a surprise for mum and dad.

Along the way Galya described how it had all happened.

It turned out that immediately after my departure Vasily Stolbov had sent my mother a letter in which he mentioned in detail how I had acquitted myself in the unit, how respected I was by my regimental buddies, and what date I had set off home. But he could not have foreseen that I would be delayed for a week for the reformatting of the documents. This introduced an element of confusion into mum's calculations. But, having received the letter, she went straight to the enlistment office and found out the timetables for all the trains passing through Uralsk with demobilised soldiers aboard, worked out roughly when I would arrive, and for six days, and nights went to meet every military train, in the hope that today would be the day. But I did not turn up. mum was in despair; by all calculations I should have arrived. And on 6 August she was unable to get away from work. At the last moment she asked Galya to go to meet the next train just in case.

Galya and I went into the city, where our 'carriage' awaited us – an ancient horse harnessed to a gig that was just as venerable. We tossed our things into the cart. Galya and I walked up the middle of the road and chatted. It was hot, there was not a cloud in the sky, and the sun was beating down, as on the warmest summer days. And it was dusty as well; there had evidently not been rain for a long time.

Uralsk was a small provincial city. Earlier it had been called Yaitsk and it was the domain of the Yaik Cossacks. It stood on the bank of the Ural river. Once deep and turbulent, the river had grown shallow over time, although the current remained strong and vigorous. When I was a child my friends and I used to love 'travelling to Europe' and back; for this, one only needed to cross the Ural river which divided Europe and Asia, or walk across the bridge to the opposite bank. I also enjoyed wandering down our main street, Soviet Street, and tirelessly looking at the memorial plaques on the walls of the houses. They told you a lot, in particular that our city had been visited by Alexander Pushkin, Leo Tolstoy, Vladimir Dal, Alexei N. Tolstoy and Dmitry Furmanov, that Mikhail Frunze and Vasily Chapaiev had fought here, and Emilyan Pugachov had been married here.

At the time when the events described took place Uralsk was not a very developed city. The buildings were mainly one-storeyed and wooden; only in the centre were there brick buildings of three or four floors, some remaining from old times, others put up during the Soviet era. There were no asphalt roads and public transport was poorly developed. But on that day when I walked home from the station almost the length of the entire city, it seemed to me to be a wonderful place. It was my home town, which I had always loved. As in most small cities, life was peaceable, open and unhurried. And the people living there were unpretentious and considerate.

Today Uralsk is on the other side of a border – in the independent sovereign state of Kazakhstan. It is difficult to imagine that this immemorially Russian city, in which all my relatives had been born and grown up, where my childhood and youth had been spent, has now become an alien, foreign place. Back then in 1945 nobody could have foreseen this . . .

I walked over my native soil, greedily breathing in the air, which was permeated by sun, greenery and dust and took pleasure in knocking the dirt off my soldiers' boots.

And finally, we arrived. I had not actually lived here. In my absence, my parents had rented two small rooms in a private house with a kitchen and a separate entrance. My heart stood still as I opened the wicket gate and entered the large yard. Galya took me to our half of the house. Coming to meet me was my new 'grandmother', Anna Ivanovna Malyutina. It was she who had looked after my mother when she had come to work at the Cheka as a sixteen-year-old girl in 1920. They took her on as a courier, while my 'grandmother' worked as a cleaner and janitor. In winter mum would run all over town in her crêpe de chine skirt, soldiers' boots and short coat, which her colleagues had gathered up for her, and when she came home, 'grandmother' would say: 'Get onto the stove and warm yourself up, Shura.' She would bring hot water and talk to her kindly. Then 'grandmother' got married and moved to another city. Mum remembered Anna Ivanovna and told me about her. And then one day when I was at the front, mum met her on the street. It turned out that she had lost her husband, then her daughter, ended up on her own, and come back to her niece in Uralsk. The niece had squeezed the old woman's money out of her and was now trying to expel her from the house. Anna Ivanovna burst into tears as she described this. Mum invited her to live with us. 'My daughter's at the front and my husband and I are on our own. You can be a mother to me and a grandmother to my daughter when she comes home.' Indeed, I did call her 'grandmother'. She was a wonderful old woman, kind and useful around the home. We soon forgot that she was not related to us.

It was Anna Ivanovna who met me on the threshold of our home. I greeted her, dropped my things and ran off to see my mother at work. When I ran up to the Party city committee building, where my mother worked, she was already coming down the stairs to meet me. I cannot describe what followed: whether we cried, or laughed or simply kept silent, as we vigorously hugged each other. Maybe it was a bit of everything. That meeting on the staircase has disappeared into a fog.

It turned out that when our landlady's daughter saw a girl in army uniform entering the yard, she immediately guessed that it was my mother's long-awaited daughter. Though very unwell, with a temperature of almost 39 degrees, she had risen from her bed and run to tell my mother the joyful news of my arrival.

So, mum and I set off for home. In our absence 'grandmother' had warmed some water and placed a trough in the kitchen. You can imagine how blissful it was to wash off the many days of grime from the carriage! Mum got out my favourite dress from before the war. I put it on, tightly, tugging the belt army style. My mother laughed: 'Yulia, you're not in the army now.' Then my father arrived and mum informed him of my return. We sat at the table, with a festive tablecloth, vodka and some modest cold cuts.

'Have a smoke,' said my father, reaching for his cigarette case.

'I don't smoke, Dad.'

'Good for you!'

He poured an almost full glass of vodka and handed it to me.

'Let's drink to your return, girl.'

'Let's drink to it, Dad.'

'Bottoms up?'

'Bottoms up.'

'Well done!'

Of course, the first toast was to me, to my return, to my good health. Then – to Victory and, as was the custom, to Stalin.

And so I was home with my beloved parents. Alive, in good health and boundlessly happy. I was only nineteen and a half years old, and I had my whole life ahead of me. Back then I did not yet appreciate what an important and memorable stage in my life had concluded. Now I consider that that was the most significant part of my life.

According to the rules in force back then I was obliged to go to the enlistment office immediately on my return home and register. I went there within a day or two. I cleaned myself up, ironed everything, and polished up my much-travelled boots. When I arrived, I was invited into an office. Behind a desk sat a tired looking officer, no longer young and, by all signs, a front-line soldier. I told him that I had come to report following demobilisation and handed him my documents. He looked attentively at the papers and surveyed me from head to toe.

'So, you're a sniper?'

'I am.'

'Do you want to be removed from the army list or kept on it?'

'Taken off, of course.'

'The point is,' he began to explain to me, 'that being a sniper is a military profession subject to special control, and I am obliged to enter you on the list.'

I remained silent and stood there, shifting my weight from one foot to the other. He took another look at me, at my artificial leather boots and my faded tunic, and sighed:

'Had a tough time?'

'I have.'

'Very well,' the officer sighed again, 'I'm not supposed to, but I'll take you off the list. I wish you a quiet life, Junior Sergeant.'

He made the appropriate entry in my Red Army booklet, stamped it, and returned the documents. I leapt out onto the street ready to shout, jump and laugh for joy. I stood for a while on the porch, took off my epaulettes, and stuffed them in my pocket. It was over. From now on I was free! I had left the army, but for many years I retained towards it a feeling partly of warmth but also of trepidation.

I cannot deny that I had come back from the war a completely different person. It wasn't just that my character had changed, but I had become more independent, decisive and motivated. The main thing was that I had learned to look at life in a different way, come to value everything around me. It seemed back then that with the defeat of Fascism the era of war would be over, that now the entire world would live in peace and tranquillity. So, like many of those in my age group, I was filled with a sensation of happiness.

CHAPTER 9

The Eternal Flame

The years went by. After the war I completed schooling in Uralsk, then attended the Lenin State Education Institute in Moscow. This was followed by work as secretary of the Frunze district committee of the Young Communist League in Moscow, then as a school headteacher in the same district, and subsequently for the Party city committee.

I strove to forget everything to do with the war. I did not like talking about the war and did not show my photographs from the war years to anyone. I burnt all the letters which I had sent home from the front as well as those I had received from regimental comrades once I was home. I destroyed the exercise book containing my own verse, much of it about the war. Over the entire post-war period I have not once picked up a rifle, although, in view of my wartime past, it was suggested to me a good few times that I might like to take part in shooting competitions. They did not understand me and I had no wish to explain that I could not and did not want to shoot any more, and was tired of all that. I even tried to forget the girls I had trained with at sniper school and fought with, girls I had always admired.

However, the war would not leave me alone, and constantly visited my dream world. They were very bad dreams, and they tormented me for over thirty years. Most commonly I dreamt that I had been taken prisoner, and each time the same dream repeated itself: two Nazis grabbed me by the arms and took me down a staircase. I was brought into a cellar and there, lying face down on the floor lay one of our soldiers, but dressed for some reason in a scarlet silk shirt. One of the torturers would go up to him and apply a burning torch to his back, the shirt would begin to smoulder and turn black at the edges. The soldier would remain silent. I would look on this with horror and think: 'I can't take this.'

One other dream was also repeated with frightening regularity. Our regiment is encircled. I see the advancing Nazis and begin to run, looking for somewhere I can safely conceal my Red Army booklet and Young Communist League membership card, so they don't fall into enemy hands. I keep running, and look around, but I can't find a suitable place. The Nazis are getting closer and closer and I dash about, not knowing where to put my documents. I cry out in a loud voice, and this cry would often waken not just me, but the rest of the family. Waking up was difficult after dreams like that. I would frequently wake up in a sweat with my heart beating violently and for the rest of the day I would not be able to rid myself of these frightening sensations.

1965! Twenty years since the day of the Soviet people's victory in the Great War for the Fatherland. For the first time the nation was preparing to mark this truly great celebration on a broad countrywide scale.

Why for the first time?

Stalin had not lived to see the first ten-year jubilee; he died in 1953. After his death the state was headed for a short time by Georgy Malenkov and Nikolai Bulganin, and then in 1954 power fell into the hands of Nikita Khrushchev, who had served up until then as first secretary of the Ukrainian Communist Party central committee and of the Soviet Communist Party's Moscow city committee. Different people had different views of him, and that is still the case today. I am inclined to agree with those who regard Khrushchev as the man who knocked the first brick out from the country's foundation. Khrushchev did a lot of damage both politically and economically. It was he who abolished the most important, the most beloved, celebration of the people – Victory Day – as a countrywide state celebration. His motivation was simplistic: we should not, he claimed, humiliate other nations by constantly reminding them of their defeat and our Victory. He was incapable of realising that by this decision he humiliated his own people, who had borne huge losses for the sake of victory and saved not only their own country, but also the whole of Europe from enslavement. Under Khrushchev, 9 May once again became an ordinary working day and no major formal measures were officially conducted.

It was hurtful and offensive . . . But everyone, including front-line veterans, silently swallowed this pill and came to terms with it. We quietly put up with everything that state power, both then and now, inflicted on us, and submitted to it. As a result, we have what we have.

And so, they attempted to deprive us of Victory celebrations. But this did not prevent the people from marking this outstanding anniversary every year. Regimental comrades met up again; veterans came to Moscow from all over the USSR. Families gathered, for the war had affected every family, every individual, in one way or another. The occasion was also celebrated within many work teams and at institutes of learning. When I became a school headteacher, I decided that the children ought to be familiar with and honour this occasion, and therefore we began to celebrate it. I well remember that day, 9 May 1957. Lessons were not cancelled; I had no right to do that. However, all the pupils were in their best clothes, the teachers were also festively attired, and war veterans wore the ribbons representing their decorations on their chests. The whole school was gathered in the assembly hall, with the staff on the stage. I was the main speaker.

Announcements were made by the senior Pioneer leader, Valya Slivochkina. I can still hear her voice: 'The next speaker veteran front-line soldier . . .' I looked round, searching for a guest I was unaware of, wondering why I had not been notified that someone was coming. But Valya continued: 'Sniper . . .' I still didn't guess who she was talking about, 'and current school headmistress Yulia Konstantinovna Zhukova.' Good heavens, it was me they were so solemnly referring to. We had not arranged it like this and therefore I was surprised, and a little bewildered. The hall rang with applause. My preparation for my short address had been lengthy and thorough; I had selected facts and examples which could not fail to touch and move the children. I put all my passion into my speech. And at the end I proposed (though I hadn't meant to do so): 'I ask you to honour the memory of the fallen with a minute's silence.' From the stage it was clearly visible how the rows of children started, then drew themselves up again and froze still. There was absolute silence in the hall. It seemed that nobody was even breathing. And my own throat was choked with emotion.

Afterwards the most senior teacher in the school, V. I. Derzhavina, came up to me and said that her spirits had dropped when I proposed that they should honour the memory of the fallen. 'Our children have not been used to it. It's always noisy at ordinary assemblies; nobody listens to anyone. I was afraid that someone would laugh or make an inappropriate comment. That would have been awful! I congratulate you; I am simply amazed.'

After Khrushchev was removed, Victory Day was once again declared a state celebration.

And so, on 9 May 1965, Red Square saw the first military parade dedicated to the anniversary of Victory. I was lucky enough to attend that parade as an invited guest. The spectator stands were filled with people. The troops were drawn up on the square. The fanfare sounded, then came greetings on behalf of the country's leadership, and the parade began. For the first time since that memorable parade on 24 June 1945, the Victory banner was borne out onto the square and among the group who carried it were Heroes of the Soviet Union Mikhail Yegorov and Meliton Kantaria, who had erected this banner on the Reichstag in Berlin. Military units and cadets of military academies, from the Suvorov and Nakhimov colleges, filed past in a triumphal march. Then came the latest military technology. Bringing up the rear was a mass brass band. The Party and government leaders left their place on top of Lenin's mausoleum.

Everything was majestic, beautiful and impressive. But back then, and when I recall that parade now, it seems to me that there was something incomplete about it, as if some element was lacking or something important omitted. I don't know what the problem was, but I was probably not the only one who had a similar sensation. It was no accident that after the parade was over the people did not disperse for a long time, but remained in the stands, as if expecting something. Only after a few minutes, diffidently at first and then more boldly, they began to go out onto the square, gathered in groups, shared jokes, laughed and took photos. This went on for a long time. Whatever way it came about, a feeling of festivity, joy and enthusiasm overtook everyone.

A memorial medal was forged for the Victory jubilee. Then further medals were established for the thirtieth, fortieth and fiftieth anniversaries of Victory. They were awarded not only to veterans, but also to those who were in military service during the jubilee year.

Another ten years went by. For me what happened in 1975 blocked out everything for a long time and filled my life with new interest. That year preparations for the Victory jubilee began long before the event and were organised on a very broad scale, with a great flourish. New films and plays were produced on a military theme; information about the war and participants in it was regularly printed in newspapers and magazines; there were festivals, competitions, conferences, walks around places of military distinction, lessons in patriotism, memorial vigils, and many, many other functions. The twenty-episode Soviet–American documentary film *The Unknown War* ran on television for almost two months. All this helped to create a particular mood in society.

And the thing that I had so strenuously and laboriously avoided right through the post-war years came to pass: I began to think about the war more frequently. I recalled the training at sniper school, the girls, and the various episodes of life at the front. The names of my regimental comrades and friends at the Central Women's Sniping School surfaced in my memory. Photos of the war years were taken out of the suitcase, along with my forage cap and epaulettes. I would often take them in my hands and examine them. A feeling of delayed regret arose in my heart – regret that I had excised my front-line friends from my memory. The war returned to my dreams more and more often; I kept dreaming of retreat, encirclement, the fear of being captured . . . These memories began to make me nervous.

One day I had a phone call from a fellow student in my year at the institute of education, Svetlana Gordaya, whom I had met many years after graduation and made friends with.

'You know what: I heard on the radio that the women snipers are having a reunion somewhere.'

'Who? Where?'

'I don't know – in some park.'

'In some park? When?'

'I don't know that either. I only caught the end of the broadcast. I don't know any more.'

I had to find out! Immediately! But how? Where would I start? Who could I inquire from? I did not know what to do. Nobody I asked had heard anything about it. My friend Galya Kazakova had also heard it on the radio in passing, but was unable to help me. I got incredibly upset; here was a real chance to find some of the girls, but it was not working out.

That's the way things happen in life: for so many years I had not wanted even to think about those times, and now suddenly I was gripped by an insuperable desire just to see anyone at all from my military past. I sometimes tried to imagine what our reunion would be like, but my imagination proved inadequate – it all seemed so unreal.

February 20th, 1975 has stuck in my memory for ever. I was sitting at my desk in my office, when I opened the newspaper *Komsomol Pravda*, looked through the first article, and turned the page. On the second page an article entitled 'sniper' immediately caught my eye. Without suspecting anything, I began to read. And suddenly ... It was about our sniper school! About its graduates! I was barely able to read to the end. It turned out that a council of veterans from the school had long been active and the former cadets and instructors were meeting almost every year.

With fingers trembling from excitement I dialled the telephone number of the editorial office and inquired how to telephone the article's author, G. Alimova. I immediately rang her and incoherently explained that I was also at the sniper school, that I had found out about the reunions from her article, and I would like to be put in touch with someone. She gave me the phone number of Nina Solovyei, chairwoman of the council of school veterans. I immediately rang her and found out that there would be a reunion of graduates from our school in June in honour of the thirtieth anniversary of Victory. Whereas only graduates of the first two cohorts had been invited to previous reunions, it had now been decided to involve everyone who had attended the Central Women's Sniping School.

What a commotion followed! I think all my friends, acquaintances, fellow workers and neighbours knew that I had found my girls, that there would soon be a reunion, and they would be coming from all the Soviet republics. It did not matter to me that I had not seen anybody yet and did not even know who would be coming and whether any of those I knew and remembered would be there. The important thing was that I now had some hope of finding the girls. At the request of the school veterans' council chair, I also sent out invitations, helped to track people down, and negotiated with regard to excursions. And all this time I was incredibly excited. My agitation infected others. At work I was constantly asked: 'Well, how's it going?' to say nothing of those at home.

I began to count down the days to the reunion. The night before that special day I got out my light-coloured best costume and pinned to the lapel all my decorations, which I would be wearing tomorrow for the first time in thirty years. I didn't seem to have forgotten anything. The main thing was to take two handkerchiefs, just to be on the safe side. I put my wartime photos in my bag.

And finally, it arrived, 7 June, the day of the reunion. I got up early and left home with my heart beating resonantly and my legs literally giving way beneath me from the excitement. I took a bus, then the underground. I observed people taking note of my decorations – it was unusual to see them. On the bus some man respectfully gave up his seat. Then it was down to the Izmailov underground station. I got out of the carriage and awaiting me on the platform were Svetlana Gordaya and her husband Sergei Putyayev, who were going with me.

Sergei was also a front-line veteran who had left for the war while still a boy and spent the war years in the 21st Army. That day he was still unaware that within a year or two he would locate the veterans' council for his own army and would be as excited as I was that day when he first went to a reunion with his friends in combat. He realised what that reunion meant to me and therefore he had brought a camera to take some snaps as mementos.

We walked quickly across the park, almost running. I was getting agitated. 'What if we're late?' What if I don't know anyone. After all, it's been thirty years. And what if they don't recognise me? What sort of reunion would that be? And what if no one turns up?

Finally, we reached the meeting point, on the park's main thoroughfare, and saw that they were already lining up. There were lots of our graduates, at least 350–400, all dressed up, with their military decorations, happy and animated, all talking loudly and laughing. Our girls! I became even more agitated: how would I find anyone in this tumult? And then suddenly I heard: 'Yulia, Yulia's here!' It was Asya Molokova, who was the first to recognise me. I looked, and there they were, my dear girls! Older, looking different, but it was them all the same! I ran over to them. Strange as it may seem, I immediately recognised everyone standing there. However, in my agitation all their names, which I had striven to recall, vanished from my memory. I took some photos out of my bag and pointed at them with my finger: here *you* are, and that's *you*, and this is *you*. I couldn't fit names to them. Only later, when I had calmed down a bit, was everything restored and the names came back to me. And after initial hugs and kisses Galya Barannikova told her twelve-year-old daughter who had come to the reunion with her: 'Ira, this is the very same Yulia Zhukova I told you so much about, whose letters and verse we have been keeping for thirty years now.' And Ira began to read my verse, which I no longer remembered myself.

We lined up somehow or other, six in a row and, led by a military band (as at the school!), the column moved off towards the statue of Lenin, where flowers were laid. Then came the laying of wreaths and a minute's silence at Victory Square. Suddenly Anya Vereshchagina, who was walking beside me, leaned over and whispered: 'Yulia, there's a woman behind us. Her face is very familiar, but I can't remember her name.' I turned around and recognised Masha Duvanova! We rushed towards each other, embraced and stayed in that position for a long time. The column went on and on, engulfing us on both sides. Someone beside us gave a sob – it was Olya Orlova, who had also been one of Masha's charges, but from the preceding cohort. The three of us then dashed off to catch up with the column.

A formal assembly took place in the outdoor theatre. It was attended by the secretary of the Young Communist League central committee, Boris Pastukhov, Chairwoman Zinayida Fyodorova of the Soviet women's committee, a woman poet from Iran, representatives of military units in which our graduates had served, and a group of Pioneers. The school banner was borne in and everyone stood up. The Soviet national anthem was played and followed by greetings and recollections. Due reverence was paid to the memory of those who had lost their lives. There were a lot of girls who had not lived to see Victory. From a report at this reunion I learned that, of the 1,885 graduates from our sniper school who ended up at the front, over 250 were killed in the course of fulfilling military assignments. That is a lot, but ours was one of the most dangerous professions.

After the ceremonies were over, we wandered around the park for a long time, took photos and talked, talked non-stop, as if we wanted to make up for everything we had missed out on over the previous thirty years. Our lives had been shaped in different ways, but we all had families, work and dwelling places. Only now do you begin to realise how wonderful it is to have everything you need for a normal, calm, life. Back then this seemed so natural! Generally speaking, nobody complained about life. The subsequent biographies of some of them simply staggered me.

One of those in our section was Anya Tarasova. Small, skinny, taciturn and timid, she always followed her friends' wishes without protest – that was how I remembered her at school. But after the war she had a very successful career as a military instructor at a male college and a successful marriage, giving birth to six children. Not bad for a shrinking violet!

Also surprising, but on a different level, was the fate of Masha Logunova – our extraordinarily strict but fair sergeant-major. She always gave me the impression of being a highly literate, educated person. It turned out that after the war she had been unable to continue her studies and, left without a profession, she took a job as a bath attendant. True, she did not complain about life either and was happy with her husband and children. However, I struggled to recognise her. In place of our dashing sergeant-major who made the whole company tremble, there stood before me a very middle-aged-looking, modestly dressed woman. If I had not been told that this was Masha Logunova, I would never have guessed. But she recognised me and we greeted each other very warmly, as indeed was the case with everyone else, whether former cadets or school staff.

The following day excursions were organised for those taking part in the reunion. We had fourteen plush excursion coaches and made ourselves comfortable on board. In accordance with established tradition, we began with a visit to the Lenin Mausoleum and placed wreaths on the tomb of the Unknown Soldier. Then, for a long time afterwards, we gathered in groups, enjoyed strolling round Red Square, recalled the past and talked about our current lives. Sergei took a lot of photos. As always, there were many tourists wandering round the square and they looked at us with undisguised curiosity. One quite elderly woman came up, took me by the hand and, glancing at my decorations, asked something in her own language. Not knowing how to explain it to her, I just said: 'The war.' 'Oh!' she said, raising her eyebrows; apparently, she understood. Looking me in the eye, she firmly squeezed my hand once more.

We were then taken to the hostel of the Higher Young Communist League College, where those who had come from out of town were accommodated. This building was erected after the war in the place where the first sniper course had been held – a course which became the basis for our school. One of the nearby thoroughfares is called Snayperskaya ulitsa ('Sniper Street') and another is named in honour of Hero of the Soviet Union Alia Moldagulova.

After dinner we wandered through the various rooms, all in our own groups. Our squad, headed by Masha Duvanova, cosily ensconced itself in one of the rooms. Once again there was no end to the chatter; the most frequently heard phrase was: 'Remember how . . . ?' Suddenly the door flew open wide and in came, or practically flew, a hysterical Milya Dogadkina. It turned out that, amongst the huge masses of people who had come for the reunion, we had not spotted each other, and now she had learned completely by chance about the arrival of such a large group from our squad and was very upset that she had not met us straight away and thus wasted the whole day. We were barely able to calm her down.

We then took another stroll somewhere. As if afraid that we might lose one another, we kept constantly together and – in the literal sense of the term – held hands.

The reunion went on for three days. Excursions around Moscow and visits to the best museums and theatres were organised for the participants.

All this time I wandered around as if in a different world. I returned home in a dreadful state of excitement. My brain was crowded with impressions and I talked incessantly, not allowing anyone to get a word in. And I slept poorly.

Then came the farewell dinner. We arrived a little before the set time and assembled in a neighbouring square. We were standing there, talking, when a woman came up to our group and asked who we were and why we had gathered here. We explained. Then, literally with tears in her eyes, she said: 'I have a daughter. On behalf of her and myself I would like to say thank you very much for protecting us, for everything you did for us.' We ended up in tears ourselves, of course.

There have been a number of occasions when I have encountered manifestations of respect for our military past. I was heading for some celebratory function one day with my full regalia of decorations, when a man came up to me and asked permission to kiss my hand – 'In token of your feats,' he said. Another time a middle-aged woman approached and bowed low before me. I was unable to go on my way without talking to her. It turned out that her husband had lost his life in the war and she had been left completely on her own. There were occasions when complete strangers gave me flowers in the street. I realised that in this way they were voicing their respect not for me personally, but through me, for all front-line veterans.

At work I never talked about my life at the front and therefore my co-workers and, in particular, my colleagues from other departments, knew almost nothing about my wartime past. And when one of the speakers at a formal gathering in 1975 talked a little bit about me, everyone was surprised and the next day at work not one of them passed me without voicing their respect.

But later on it was different. I remember returning home from an anniversary parade on Red Square with my decorations on my jacket. I was walking along the street and a pretty young woman was coming towards me. She looked at my decorations and spitefully commented through gritted teeth: 'Giving them an airing . . .' I felt bitter about it, but was nonplussed and could not come up with a suitable reply. That day I was going to see my comrade, front-line veteran Vasya Ryabtsev, whose wartime friends traditionally gathered at his place. One of them was an air force pilot, who had received many very high awards. But, instead of the orders and medals with which I usually saw him, he had on this occasion merely attached his medal ribbons to his jacket. Seeing that everyone else was in full regalia, he attempted to explain. 'What are you frightened of?' I asked him. He remained silent. This was the time of *Perestroika* and the 'reformers' were in a hurry to rewrite history and to overthrow former authorities and heroes. Not everyone could withstand the pressure, not even this brave aviator.

But this was some time away. Back then in 1975 nobody yet knew that the time would come when war veterans would be subjected to insults and stop wearing their wartime decorations.

On the final day of the reunion we gathered for a farewell dinner in a huge hall, with splendidly laid tables, delicious food, and drinks for every taste. Our group cordially agreed that our bottles of strong drink should be replaced by water and kvass. It was incredibly noisy in the hall. At every table people were bringing up memories, discussing them, and singing their old songs. Then the entire hall roared out what had been the most popular song at the school, 'Daydreams'. It's a quite unpretentious song, but we loved it and sang it both on the march and off-duty.

> The nightingale's beloved song is mine,
> A heart-felt song that makes my spirit pine.
> I wallow in day-dreams of mere confection,
> But youth flies by without love or affection.
> I cannot understand at all what's driving us apart.
> At night I clutch my tear-soaked pillow tightly to my
>   heart
> There's music at the window and the moon glows at
>   night,
> But believe me, beloved:
> Our paths are not to cross.

The chorus of 400 voices was a mighty sound!

After supper we walked to the underground station and sang our favourite songs from the school. We said goodbye at the station. It was a long time before we could bear to part. The girls went their different ways. We swapped addresses and promised that we would keep in touch, write to one another. We were in tears, of course. I reckon that during these few days I saw more women's tears than I had seen in a year and a half of army service.

Two weeks later Sergei rang to say that he had printed out almost 250 photographs for my friends. Well done! And so quickly! It turned out that he had been so moved by our reunion that he wanted to give us the pleasure of seeing his photos as soon as possible. I really enjoyed putting them in big envelopes and sending them all over the Soviet Union – from Leningrad to Vladivostok. How happy the girls were!

Today I look at the photographs and feel the joy of our reunion once again – my first reunion after almost thirty years of anonymity. Just think: to see their wartime friends, people no longer young had travelled long distances to the capital. They came with their children, husbands and relatives, from all ends of the Soviet Union, from the various Union republics. In our squad alone, there were women from Alma-Ata, Frunze, Chita, Pavlodar, Novosibirsk, Vladivostok, Yaroslavl, Kuibyshev, Kalinin, and Kustanai.

Today many of these cities are no longer on the map, or rather, the cities remain, but their names have changed, and some are now in the so-called 'near abroad'.

I would like to mention in particular that when it came to organising sniper school reunions the central committee of the Young Communist League played the most active role. Our school was the child of the Young Communist League and the heads of the central committee did not forget it. Veterans in various places were assisted by local community organisations, which even doled out money for trips and offered supplementary leave.

The years went by and we met many times again. In 1978 the reunion held to mark the thirty-fifth anniversary of the sniper school's establishment was attended by over 500. The 376 graduates were accompanied by 120 relatives and 75 children and grandchildren. I write this with such confidence because during the reunion I jotted down on a pad everything that struck me as important and interesting. These figures are taken from that pad.

The girls later visited our home, where they always got a warm and friendly reception. On one visit Masha Duvanova and I went to Silikatnaya station, which was so familiar to us. After the war the Central Women's Sniping School premises were returned to the local Silikatnaya factory as a club building. There is a memorial plaque on it. In one of the rooms (Masha and I thought it was where our squad was lodged) an exhibition devoted to the sniper school had been opened. People walked around, had a look, recalled the events and experienced them once again. Completely by chance we met the Party organiser of one of the factory workshops. It turned out that his elder sister had been friends with one of the cadets at our school and told him a lot about us. He remembered it all, treated us with great warmth, took us through the building where we had earlier lived and told us in detail about the activities of the factory and the club.

Another time I took Masha to the Central Museum of the USSR Armed Forces, where a surprise awaited me: in one of the halls I saw the Banner of our own 611th Regiment. I was so moved that I felt like bowing the knee to it, as in earlier times. But there were people all around, so I simply stood beside it in silence. My feelings were comprehensible only to those who had been through the army and the war, sworn an oath before the Banner, and sincerely believed in the cause they were defending.

I placed a high value on our reunions and always awaited them eagerly. Afterwards I would long recall who was there, what we talked about, where we were and what we saw. Every such reunion was like a bridge back to our wartime youth; most of all we talked about that time and sang the old songs. And each time we experienced an enormous feeling of happiness that we had survived, lived through it, and seen one another again. We became almost like family.

I also regularly met friends I had fought alongside from the 88th Division in the 31st Army. I remember that at one of these army reunions there were almost 1,200 people. Some came with their husbands or wives, children and grandchildren. All the visitors were accommodated in one of the most comfortable and prestigious hotels – the Rossiya. They lived and had their meals there. All that was affordable back then, even for pensioners.

There is one incident in particular which testifies how highly the veterans valued their front-line fraternity. One of the army reunions was attended by an invalid who had come from a long way away. He had one leg and walked with crutches. He said that following shell-shock he had lost his memory, forgotten everything and could not remember which unit he served in. He heard on the radio about a reunion of 31st Army veterans and decided for some reason that that was where he had served. So he packed and went. After lengthy questioning it emerged that he had fought on a completely different front. The soldier was distraught, but then asked: 'Do you mind me coming to your reunions if I can't find my own unit?'

After the 1975 reunion my friends and I kept in touch, corresponded regularly, and for every celebration I sent off thirty or forty letters and cards and received just as many back. Even the post-lady once commented that nobody in our building had as much correspondence as I did. News from friends always brought me pleasure. But I was still in thrall to an insane passion for destroying papers and, as a result, not a single one of the many hundreds of letters I received has survived. Now I endlessly reproach myself. For they were not just letters; they were the documentary records of a dying generation describing people during the war, their lives, thoughts and feelings. And now hardly anyone writes any more; it is expensive, they are not in the mood, and illness has got the better of them.

During those years everything seemed to be developing well. Attitudes to war veterans were different. They were respected, supported, invited to contribute to the education of young people in a spirit of patriotism. Museums and displays of military glory were set up at institutes of learning and factories, meetings with participants in the war, lessons in patriotism, walks around battle sites and memorial vigils became a tradition.

And then everything fell apart . . .

Many dubious conjectures and falsehoods about the war of 1941–45 are being spread. When I read and listen to all these fabrications, I am shocked by the immoral and unprincipled nature of their authors. Yes, it is quite possible that the country's leadership during those years made major miscalculations and errors. It is possible that the cost of victory was too high, although not all researchers agree with this verdict. But the entire world has acknowledged our victory; the entire world admired the feats of the Soviet people, who saved humanity from Fascism; the entire world paid due tribute to Stalin as an outstanding figure of his time. What is the point of us belittling the role of the multinational Soviet people in the defeat of German Fascism? What is the point of composing more and more fables about the mediocrity of the Soviet war leaders and the immorality of our soldiers, thereby humiliating veterans of the war? What is it that encourages scholars, writers and all those interested in the problems of the 1941–45 war artificially to inflate the losses of the Red Army during this war?

I am convinced that for millions of our citizens the Great War for the Fatherland remains a sacred topic, one that is still soaked in red blood, for it touched almost every family. My assessment of this is based not just on my own case but also on my friends and their relatives. Therefore, we should take a more cautious attitude to everything connected with that war. However, throughout the years of *Perestroika* there were active efforts to re-evaluate the results of the war, frequently using dishonest arguments and plainly manipulating facts.

A favourite topic of the falsifiers of history is our losses in the last war. At times these 'researchers' give casualty figures which generally exceed the numbers who took part in the fighting over the four years of war. However, the Krivosheyev commission, comprising scholars, independent military historians and experts who painstakingly studied the appropriate documents, including archive material, concluded in a report published in 1993 that in the war of 1941–45 our irreplaceable losses of servicemen (killed, died from wounds and illness, missing, unreturned from captivity) came to 8.8 million. This is a little more than the total losses of the enemy (Germans as well as their allies who fought on our territory – Italians, Romanians, Hungarians, Finns, Spanish, and so on). However, a study undertaken in 2008 by the Central Defence Ministry assessed our killed and missing as 14.2 million and the hysteria over our inordinately high losses has yet to cease.

One thing is certain: the Germans waged war not just for victory, but to annihilate everything on our land: its people, including the civilian population, and its economy and culture. Suffice it to remember that losses among the civilian population were over twice as high as those among military personnel and are estimated to come to around 19 million. The blame for this falls first and foremost on the Nazis. Thus, in my view, it is inappropriate to humiliate the country and its army by waving around crude figures of casualties.

There are other 'revelations'. For instance, some maintain that, in their urge for world domination, the leaders of the Soviet Union planned to attack Germany first and then conquer other

European countries. Germany supposedly beat us to it by two or three weeks, and attacked our country first. Military historians have published refutations and produced evidence to prove that this version of events is untrue. It doesn't help. And it doesn't help that everyone sees what they want to see.

There is in this regard a different, less popular, version of events, according to which Stalin, fearing that, with further expansion of the empire, he would not be able to retain power in his hands, deliberately provoked a German attack on the Soviet Union.

Despite the contradiction between these two misrepresentations, they are both 'alive and well'. But very rarely, as far as I know, do the media publish the alternative view, that, if the Soviet Union had attacked Germany first when a good half of Europe was occupied by the Nazis, the world would have welcomed this action and humanity would have borne significantly fewer losses. But this did not happen; our country was not the first to act. This could not have happened because, as is now widely known, the USSR was not ready for war for a whole range of reasons, both objective and subjective. Thus, what talk can there be of a preventative attack by our country on Germany?

Those of us who went through the war are very often referred to as the lost generation; in other words, the majority of this generation failed to find an appropriate place in life and ended up being rejected by society. True, in the ranks of yesterday's front-line soldiers there were quite a few who were unable to adapt fully to new conditions and to organise their lives as they would have wished. But one cannot generalise on this basis. The majority of veterans who returned home immediately engaged actively in work and study and began to raise families. Often it was front-line veterans who headed for the most difficult work sectors and led public organisations. The state took care of them, supported them, rewarded them, and accorded them privileges. Society had a respectful attitude towards front-line veterans.

All this I know not from books, but from my own experience and that of my front-line friends and acquaintances, of whom I have a good number. One cannot fail to mention that many of the most respected and revered figures in society were front-line veterans, for instance: the legendary aviators and triple Heroes of the Soviet Union Alexander Pokryshkin and Ivan Kozhedub; sniper and Hero of the Soviet Union Lyudmila Pavlichenko; popular writers Konstantin Simonov and Boris Polevoi; poets Yulia Drunina and Alexander Tvardovsky, who both created works of staggering power about the war; film and theatre favourites Innokenty Smoktunovsky and Yuri Nikulin; cosmonauts Georgy Beregovoi and Konstantin Feoktistov, whose names are widely known throughout the country. They, along with hundreds, thousands, of other outstanding people, have deservedly earned the love and respect of their fellow-countrymen and women. There have also been war veterans among the country's top leadership. So, what lost generation are they talking about and why? Is it not just to humiliate the older generation one more time and deprive war veterans of their prestige as defenders of the homeland and a heroic generation of victors?

With the beginning of the reforms war veterans really began to feel uneasy about their position in society.

It was painful for us to watch the widespread development of a trade in Soviet orders and medals, military banners, and generals' and officers' uniforms – and all with the connivance of the authorities. This trade was open and ubiquitous: in shops, stalls, at markets, in underground passages, right on the streets. It was conducted by young people, boys who were speculating with the sacred treasures of their fathers and grandfathers.

Veterans stopped wearing their wartime decorations – some were embarrassed, others were scared. There were cases where veterans were insulted and even beaten up and their decorations taken for sale.

At the same time exhibits in schools dedicated to our military achievements were wrecked, literally wrecked. Tens of thousands of highly valuable exhibits were destroyed in the process – original documents, letters, photographs and the personal belongings of veterans. Common graves and memorials to Soviet soldiers were vandalised.

On 23 February 1992, several hundred former servicemen and women, war veterans, ordinary Moscow citizens, gathered to pay tribute to the memory of the fallen and to lay wreaths on the tomb of the Unknown Soldier by the Kremlin wall. The procession was moving down Tver Street, when its path was blocked by special police forces. They beat totally innocent people with batons and would not allow them through to the sacred spot. Only towards evening did several of the staunchest and most persistent of them get through to the Alexander gardens and lay wreaths at the memorial.

On 1 May 1993, the blood of war veterans was once again spilled on the streets of Moscow. Violent measures were taken that day against participants in a May Day demonstration. Around 150 war veterans were injured and one general who had gone through the whole war died there and then on the street; he could not bear the humiliation when a young police special force member insulted and pushed him.

Nor can I forget the tale of one girl who was a witness to those events. She had turned eight that year. Along with her grandmother and grandfather she had gone to the demonstration in honour of the celebration. The bloody spectacle unfolded before her very eyes. The young girl was badly shaken when she saw blood dripping from the head of a war veteran onto his military decorations.

Then there was a campaign to destroy the prestige of those who had taken part in the war, died in combat and become national heroes.

And then yet another attempt to humiliate us. In recent years a number of regional leaders have persistently pushed the idea of promoting reconciliation between the peoples of Russia and Germany by reburying the remains of Soviet and German soldiers in common graves. This means that we will have to honour alike both those who defended our country and those who came to enslave our peoples, committed atrocities, abused, hanged, shot, raped, burned and destroyed. Germany is even prepared to allocate money for this purpose.

I bear no hatred towards the German people. But I hate those who committed atrocities on our land; I cannot and will not render honour to murderers and rapists. There is no way I can lay flowers on a tomb containing the remains of dead Nazi soldiers.

For the older generation, everything happening today is very distressing and many cannot stand it. My favourite poet, Yulia Drunina, without question a strong and courageous woman, who lived through the war, committed suicide in November 1991 from a sense of powerlessness, of the impossibility of influencing events. She could not endure what the 'reformers' did to our country and its people. In verses written just before her death Yulia Drunina wrote:

> I cannot and will not witness
> My country sliding downhill.

The outstanding writer and front-line veteran Vyacheslav Kondratyev also took his own life. Like many other members of our creative intelligentsia, he greeted the start of *Perestroika* with enthusiasm. Then, in an interview, confused and hurt, Kondratyev attempted to make sense of what was happening, of the reasons why the country and its people were being broken up. He agonised and, in the end, could not stand it. It was reported in the newspapers that this defender of the Brest fortress came from afar to the city where he had fought and threw himself under a train as a gesture of protest against the policy of the current regime and the humiliating position in which the authorities had placed war veterans.

Unfortunately, there are a number of similar cases. I do not consider that this is the best form of protest, but people make their choices.

And what about our young people in this situation? It must be difficult for them to sort out. One aviator, a Hero of the Soviet Union, told me that at a meeting with senior pupils at a Moscow school he was asked: 'Did we have to exert ourselves so much in that war, display mass heroism? Wouldn't it have been better to surrender to the Germans? Then today we would live like them.' This event testifies to the fact that we have growing up a generation of young people, many of whom have not the slightest idea of the last war, of Nazi aspirations to annihilate the Soviet Union and enslave its people.

When my thoughts go back to those far-off days, I find myself amazed each time: how did we manage to hold out against all that, to overcome it, and not only withstand but defeat it?

It seems to me that we would not have withstood it if our people had not possessed a mighty strength of spirit and an unprecedented will for victory. Just think about it: the Germans were at the gates of Moscow, getting ready for a parade on Red Square, but the basic mass of Soviet people still believed that we would overcome the Nazis and did everything possible and, at times, impossible, for the front, for victory. When, during the first days of the war, Stalin spoke those words which have since become historic: 'The enemy will be beaten, the victory will be ours,' he thereby expressed the general confidence in victory and, it appears to me, his own confidence in the people.

Literally everyone, from children to old folk, rose to defend the homeland. I remember a remarkable Soviet film about the great Georgian military leader Georgy Saakadze, which includes one stunning episode. Saakadze is trying to explain comprehensibly to his young sons that Georgia's strength is in unity. He gives each of them a twig: 'Break it,' he says. They do so. Then he binds the twigs into bundles: 'Try now,' he says. They couldn't manage it. In this way Saakadze vividly illustrated to his sons that, if everyone acted together, Georgia could not be defeated.

Likewise, in our own country during those dreadful years all the people were united in our faith, hope and desire for victory: Russians and Tatars, Ukrainians and Uzbeks, Byelorussians and Kazakhs, Georgians and Kirghiz, people of every nationality. We were united in our love for our homeland. Of course, even back then there were some who were unhappy with Soviet power, but at the country's moment of danger patriotic sentiments proved stronger. It is no fiction but absolute truth that, when the war started, many people who had suffered under Soviet power and even found themselves imprisoned volunteered for the front. And they went, fought, performed feats of courage and received decorations. Particularly illustrative in this regard is a conversation which General Guderian, one of the major German military commanders, describes in his memoirs. In 1942, when our victory was still a long way away, he happened to meet and talk with a former tsarist general in some city. He was stunned by what he heard from this general: 'If you had come twenty years ago, we would have greeted you with great enthusiasm. Now it's too late. We have begun to revive . . . Now we are fighting for Russia, and in this we are united.' In this way the one-time enemy of Soviet power precisely conveyed the feeling of the people during the grim years of war.

The years go by. One by one my friends and comrades-in-arms depart this life. On the one hand, this is natural; old age, illness and wounds take their toll. And yet I am inclined to believe that, if their lives had been different over the last few years, they might still be around.

There are fewer and fewer of us. The veterans are fading away, and with them so is the war . . . It is difficult to imagine that the day will come when there will be no veterans left from the Great War for the Fatherland. But that day will inevitably come.

> When our last front-line veteran
> Shuts his eyes and lies in peace,
> Doubtless, at that moment
> We'll all feel a great unease.
> The heart of every Russian
> Will be struck by a strange malaise.
> If the sun's out brightly shining,
> It will yield to a darkening haze.
> We'll feel an untimely shudder,
> We'll sense a feverish glow,
> And the maple in mother's garden
> Will suddenly bow down low.

(From Nikolai Berezovsky, 'The Last Front-Line Veteran')

The front-line veterans will depart and, for new generations, the Great War for the Fatherland will become just 'history'. But what will it look like to future generations? Will our heirs remember what the Soviet people did for the whole of humanity? Will they take pride in the feats of the older generations, of their fathers and grandfathers?

I hope my jottings may serve as a reminder of the events of the war of 1941–45 and the people who defended the country back then. It is my special desire that the dear girls with whom I traversed the arduous roads of war should be remembered and accorded due respect. I have no wish to divide them into those who were killed or have died since the war and those still alive. They are all still with me, all in my heart, all still alive.

Here are their names and the places they came from:

Anya Barannikova	Alma-Ata (now Almaty, Kazakhstan)
Nadya Bolshakova	Novosibirsk
Ira Chekmaryova	Leningrad (now St Petersburg)
Milya Dogadkina	Balabanovo
Dusya Filippova	Unknown
Nadya Isakova	Unknown
Sasha Khaidukova	Unknown
Masha Khelemendik	Vladivostok
Nina Kotyelnikova	Kalinin (now Tver)
Liza Lakontseva	Kuibyshev (now Samara)
Galya Lepyoshkina	Chita
Asya Molokova	Pavlodar (now in Kazakhstan)
Dusya Pogrebnaya	Lvov (now Lviv, Ukraine)
Lyuba Ruzhitskaya	Unknown
Vera Samarina	Unknown
Katya Sheiko	Kustanai Region (now Kostanay Region, Kazakhstan)
Valya Shilova	Uralsk (now Oral, Kazakhstan)
Anya Tarasova	Taldy-Kurgan Region (now in Kazakhstan)
Masha Torgova	Unknown
Anya Vereshchagina	Alma-Ata
Roza Vozina	Uralsk
Roza Yegorova	Dzhezkazgan (now Jezkazgan, Kazakhstan)
Masha Zhabko	Pavlodar

There is one more altogether shorter list – of my instructors at the Central Women's Sniping School, who did not get to fight but taught us the skills of combat and shared with us all the burdens of life at the school. Who knows how many of us survived thanks to them? I remember them and I love them.

Sergeant Masha Duvanova	Frunze (now Bishkek, Kyrgyzstan)
Senior Sergeant Tonya Skvortsova	Yaroslavl
Sergeant-Major Masha Logunova	Chelyabinsk
Second Lieutenant Irina Papikhina	Unknown

And I cannot fail to mention one more time my loyal knights in shining armour. Where they hailed from, I do not know:

Sergeant-Major Vasily Stolbov
Corporal Alexei Popov
Corporal Pyotr Chirkov

I have here named only the closest and dearest of those with whom the war brought me into contact.

As for my comrades-in-arms who lost their lives, I dedicated the following verse to them two years ago:

> Victory day and Moscow's humming.
> The storm's left puddles on the ground.
> Alone beside the Flame Eternal,
> I don't need anyone around.
> For, through the flame I see a squadron:
> My fallen friends march on their way.
> Battle-weary, ever marching
> From far-off times to present day.
> Mute but, on their doleful faces,
> Sadness, wrath, and pain I sight,
> Reproach for any who betrayed them –
> And survived the final fight.
> Head bowed, 'Forgive!' I whisper.
> I see them all still living and, anew,
> I keep repeating: 'If you can, forgive us,'
> The offered roses have a bloody hue.

They're gone. Again, I stand alone,
But through the burning flame I see
Their flaming hearts all bound together,
Ever to eternity.

Making war is not women's business but, the way things worked out, they were required to taste in full the bitter fate of a soldier. A few years ago, I read in some newspaper that over 800,000 women took part in the war as members of the services or as hired civilians. It was hard for everybody: not just infantry like us, and those who flew planes, sat in tanks, ensured communications during combat, but also those who stood at crossroads under artillery barrages, directing traffic in rain and snowstorms, summer heat and winter cold, not to mention those who carried the wounded from the field of battle, stood for days on end by operating tables, saving the lives of soldiers and officers, restoring their health, as well as those in laundry brigades who daily washed tons of filthy, sweat-soaked, blood-stained soldiers' linen.

Embedded in my memory are the words of one literary hero, a general, who reasoned roughly like this: 'If you're infantry, you should get a medal.' I would say this: 'If a woman has been at the front and taken part in combat, she should get a special order for courage, endurance and patience.' There is no question that it was hard for everybody in war, but for women it was most arduous. For the majority of women shooting, bombing raids, death, blood and human suffering are in themselves intolerable. But even harder to bear were the physical and psychological loads, the filth of trench life. And there was nobody to heed your weeping. You are not going to shed tears before those who are enduring the same privations and difficulties. And male company, in which we constantly lived, day and night, is not very well disposed to complaints and outpourings. I cannot deny that the male environment was also at times responsible for additional difficulties.

I also want to say that seeing people perish is always tough. But when those perishing are women, whom God ordained not to fight, not to perish on fields of battle, but to create and protect families, to bear and bring up children, it is even harder. And they did perish.

I am one of those 800,000 women who shared with men all the trials and horrors of war. And like all the others, I did not have an easy time. I was very keen to forget the war; I did everything to achieve that. At times it seemed to me that the war had finally disappeared from my life. But that was self-deception; I have not forgotten anyone or anything. Otherwise I would not have dreamt those frightful dreams about the war for thirty long years and I would not be able to write at such length and in such detail about my life at the front and my front-line friends. I simply strove very hard to drive thoughts about the war deeper inside me, where they slumbered and occasionally broke through to the surface, making me anxious and agitated.

And now the time has come to talk about that period. This is not easy either. The war has gripped me again. Again, I have become agitated, and agonise as I recall that stage of my life, which I regard as the most important and significant of all.

This stage concluded on 6 August 1945, when I returned to my home town of Uralsk, and a new period of life began.

The Order of Glory

Graduates of the Central Women's Sniping School who were awarded the
Order of Glory (list compiled 1976; post-war married names in brackets).

Order of Glory, 2nd Class

Artamonova (Danilovtseva), Vera Ivanovna	3rd Shock Army
Belobrova (Mironova), Nina Pavlovna	3rd Shock Army
Blagova (Zagryadskaya), Raisa Vasilyevna	3rd Shock Army
Boltaieva (Vyatkina), Antonina Nikitichna	3rd Shock Army
Bordashevskaya (Kisé), Olga Fyodorovna	Second Byelorussian Front, 204th Rifle Div.
Bykova, Olga Nikolaievna	3rd Shock Army
Golievskaya (Veletkevich), Iya Ilyinichna	3rd Shock Army
Kataieva (Bondarenko), Maria Dmitriyevna	5th Army, 430th Rifle Regt.
Leshchova (Zhirova), Lidia Nikolaievna	Second Byelorussian Front, 204th Rifle Div., 730th Rifle Regt.
Makarova, Lyubov Mikhailovna	3rd Shock Army
Shanina, Roza Yegorovna	5th Army
Vinogradova (Mikhailova), Alexandra Yevgenyevna	3rd Shock Army
Vostrukhina, Anna Yefimovna	3rd Shock Army
Yakusheva (Maryenkina), Olga Sergeyevna	3rd Shock Army
Zubchenko (Solovyova), Maria Gheorghiyevna	3rd Shock Army

Order of Glory, 3rd Class

Agapova (Nefyedova), Vera Vasilyevna	2nd Guards Army
Albert, Maria Semyonovna	33rd Army
Alpatova, Olga Petrovna	4th Shock Army
Anderman, Lidia Yakovlevna	31st Army
Avramenko (Sharapova), Roza Anatolyevna	3rd Shock Army
Baklanova (Yuryeva), Antonina Makarovna	31st Army
Bardina (Shustova), Klavdia Nikolayevna	3rd Shock Army
Belousova (Shevtsova), Marina Fyodorovna	Leningrad Front, 125th Rifle Div.
Belousova, Yulia Petrovna	3rd Shock Army
Bespalova (Gladysheva), Zoya Ivanovna	2nd Army
Bogdanova (Yermakova), Yelizavyeta Pavlovna	First Byelorussian Front
Buinova (Simonova), Maria Mikhailovna	183rd Rifle Div.
Butkova (Popova), Valentina Ivanovna	52nd Guards Rifle Div.
Chernoritskaya (Markova), Zoya Afanasyevna	10th Guards Army
Chernova (Vershinina), Zinayida Vasilyevna	31st Army, 174th Rifle Div.
Chistyokhina (Skrypkina), Larisa Mikhailovna	33rd Army, 70th Rifle Div.
Darmaros (Glebova), Tamara Gerasimovna	10th Guards Army
Dianova (Krasnoborodova), Yevdokia Fyodorovna	5th Army
Dmitriyeva, Antonina Nikolaievna	27th Army, 143rd Rifle Div.
Dobrynina (Ozerova), Anna Petrovna	48th Army
Dyomina (Isaieva), Nina Petrovna	31st Army, 174th Rifle Div.
Fedulova, Yevdokia Stepanovna	3rd Shock Army
Fomina (Demidova), Agrippina Ivanovna	2nd Baltic Front
Garanina (Frolova), Zinayida Fyodorovna	14th Army, 45th Rifle Div.
Gladysheva (Bespalova), Zoya Ivanovna	2nd Army
Gorobets (Vasilyeva), Maria Grigoryevna	Fourth Ukrainian Front
Gudovantseva, Lidia Semyonovna	1st Shock Army, 23rd Rifle Div.
Iglina (Sachkova), Klavdia Mikhailovna	Leningrad Front

Ilyina (Sysoyeva), Klavdia Ivanovna	Fourth Ukrainian Front
Ivanova (Merkulova), Valentina Afanasyevna	10th Army
Karavayeva (Kuznetsova), Antonina Nikolaievna	
	192nd Rifle Div.
Karpenko, Antonina Ivanovna	51st Army,
	204th Rifle Div.
Kashina (Shmelyova), Zinayida Mikhailovna	5th Army
Kazakevich (Gusyeva), Nina Kuzminichna	34th Army,
	182nd Rifle Div.
Kazantseva (Zhukova), Maria Innokentyevna	8th Army
Khavronina, Maria Yegorovna	27th Army
Klyetkina (Goldfeld), Yelena Shlemovna	3rd Shock Army
Knyazyeva (Izmestyeva), Irina Dmitriyevna	Fourth Ukrainian Front
Kolomytseva (Kaskova), Olga Vasilyevna	31st Army
Koltsova (Grichishkina), Maria Stepanovna	31st Army
Korotkova (Pichugina), Zoya Dmitriyevna	2nd Guards Army
Kosaya (Medynskaya), Yelena Pavlovna	47th Army
Koshelnik (Mozyarova), Nina Sergeyevna	47th Army
Kotlyarova (Zakharova), Antonina Alexandrovna	
	47nd Army
Kozhekhmetova (Galiyeva), Maria Vasilyevna	3rd Shock Army
Krasnova, Susanna Andreyevna	31st Army,
	173rd Rifle Div.
Kravchenko (Smirnova), Yelena Ivanovna	31st Army
Krokhalyova, Antonina Yefimovna	5th Army,
	159th Rifle Div.
Kuleshova, Maria Kuzminichna	31st Army
Kuvshinova, Maria Grigoryevna	315th & 173rd Rifle Divs.
Kuzmina (Podolskaya), Anna Yakovlevna	31st Army
Kuzmina, Yekaterina Ivanovna	31st Army,
	173rd Rifle Div.
Kuznetsova (Pechosheva), Natalya Yakovlevna	31st Army
Larionova (Timashova), Yekaterina Petrovna	Third Byelorussian Front
Lashchuk (Khrakovskaya), Bella Semyonovna	Third Byelorussian Front
Lashukova (Bakulyeva), Alexandra Mikhailovna	
	3rd Shock Army
Lobkovskaya, Nina Alexeyevna	3rd Shock Army

Markina, Natalya Andreyevna   Leningrad Front,
8th Army

Medvedyeva (Nazarkina), Alexandra Petrovna   31st Army,
174th Rifle Div.

Mikhailova, Polina Ivanovna   33rd Rifle Div.

Mochalova, Olga Alexeyevna   47th Army

Morozova (Ivushkina), Maria Ivanovna   31st Army

Mozharovskaya (Novikova), Yeva Andreyevna   5th Army

Mukhamyetova, Fatyma Nikolaievna   3rd Shock Army

Naumyenko (Yaryzhnova), Anastasiya Makarovna
48th Army

Nazarova (Zhibovskaya), Yekaterina Ivanovna   3rd Shock Army

Nikolaieva, Valentina Petrovna   5th Army

Novikova (Selyanina), Nadyezhda Stepanovna   5th Army

Novoseltseva (Priminina), Nina Ivanovna   48th Army,
73rd Rifle Div.

Okhotnikova (Porotnikova), Vera Filippovna   10th Guards Army

Oleinik (Birko), Serafima Isaakovna   70th Rifle Div.,
252nd Rifle Regt.

Onyanova, Lidia Andreyevna   3rd Shock Army

Pererodova (Gavrilova), Zinayida Vasilyevna   Second Byelorussian
Front

Podlazova (Nosova), Anna Leontyevna   3rd Shock Army

Polyakova (Nazarenko), Lyubov Matveyevna   31st Army

Popova (Budkova), Valentina Ivanovna   3rd Shock Army

Repina (Vlasova), Faina Fyodorovna   1st Army, 52nd Rifle Div.

Rumyantseva (Balakireva), Zinayida Vasilyevna
48th Army

Savelyeva, Klavdia Mikhailovna   2nd Guards Army

Shcholkova (Strakhova), Vera Nikiforovna   2nd Guards Army

Shkolnik, Polina Alexandrovna   3rd Shock Army

Simonovich (Trofimova)   3rd Shock Army

Smirnova (Brykovskaya), Klavdia Nikiforovna   31st Army

Sobolyeva (Kandakova), Valentina Vasilyevna   31st Army,
192nd Rifle Div.

Sokolova, Alexandra Ivanovna   27th Army

Solovei, Nina Sergeyevna   4th Shock Army

Stepanenko, Lidia Romanovna	31st Army
Suvorova, Alexandra Grigoryevna	2nd Guards Army
Syromolotova (Pustovaya), Olga Petrovna	48th Army, 217th Rifle Div.
Tanailova, Lyubov Petrovna	5th Army
Tatarinova (Gostyunina), Anna Nikolaievna	3rd Shock Army
Tregubova, Alexandra	33rd Army, 70th Rifle Div., 252nd Rifle Regt.
Tsaryova, Tamara Dmitriyevna	10th Guards Army
Tulinova (Fedchenko), Anna Yakovlevna	14th Army, 52nd Guards Rifle Div.
Ushakova (Koshevaya), Anna Andreyevna	31st Army, 173rd Rifle Div.
Vasina (Anashkina), Serafima Grigoryevna	5th Army
Vatolina (Filimonova), Zinayida Vladimirovna	3rd Shock Army, 33rd Rifle Div.
Vdovina (Bozhenova), Lidia Gheorghievna	5th Army
Velskaya (Lukasheva), Alexandra Mikhailovna	31st Army
Vershinina (Akulova), Yelena Nikolaievna	31st Army
Vidina, Antonina Sergeyevna	31st Army
Vinogradova (Kononova), Ninel Pavlovna	47th Army
Vlasova (Timofeyeva), Klavdia Vasilyevna	1st Shock Army
Yakimova Faina Stepanovna	31st Army, 174th Rifle Div.
Yerrmoshkina (Kuzovkova), Vera Ivanovna	17th Rifle Div.
Yurchenko (Lyrchikova), Yulia Alexeyevna	10th Guards Army
Zaparova, Vera Yakovlevna	31st Army, 54th Rifle Div.
Zhalnina, Vera Alexeyevna	3rd Shock Army
Zharkova, Lyudmila Andreyevna	3rd Shock Army
Zheleznikova (Rozhkova), Anna Ivanovna	31st Army
Zhuravlyova (Ivanova), Nina Alexeyevna	10th Guards Army

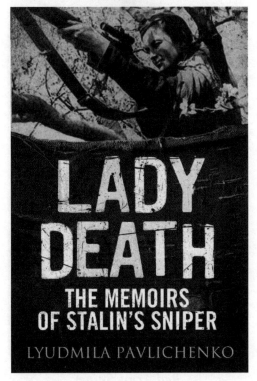

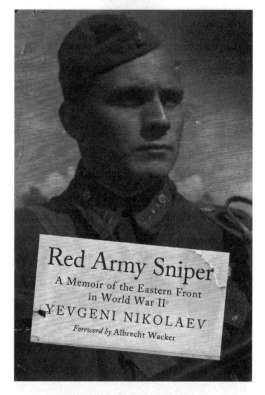

Red Army Sniper
A Memoir of the Eastern Front in World War II
Yevgeni Nikolaev
Foreword by Albrecht Wacker
ISBN: 978–1–78438–236–0